THE FUTURE IS NOW

A Beginning Guide for
Long-Range Planning
in your Church

by
Warren B. Davis
and
Richard M. Cromie

Desert Ministries Inc.
Pittsburgh

THE FUTURE
IS NOW

First Printing
Copyright MCMLXXXIV by
Desert Ministries, Inc.

ISBN 0-914733-03-6
Library of Congress Catalog Card Number:
84-72666

Scripture quotations, other than the
authors', are from the
Revised Standard Version of the Bible
copyright 1946, 1952,© 1971, 1973.

Cover Photograph copyright
Clyde Hare 1980

Printed by NorthShore Communications
Pittsburgh, Pennsylvania

*"The plans of the diligent lead surely to
abundance, but everyone who
is hasty comes only to want."*

Proverbs 21:5

*"Many are the plans in the mind of
man, but it is the purpose of the Lord
that will be established."*

Proverbs 19:21

ACKNOWLEDGEMENTS

The authors are grateful to the present Long-Range Planning Committee of Southminster Presbyterian Church in Pittsburgh, Pennsylvania, and its Chairman Donald C. Thompson, for permission to use some of the enclosed material which pertains to the recent ministry and mission of that congregation.

We also acknowledge the tremendous assistance of Eleanor B. Simpson, who typed and re-typed the manuscript, gave important advice and direction on the project, and as Executive Director of Desert Ministries, Inc., shepherded the project from the start to its completion.

We also are grateful to Mr. Richard C. Stein of NorthShore Communications of Pittsburgh, Pennsylvania for his invaluable assistance, and to Mr. Clyde W. Hare, nationally known photographer, for the cover photograph and his expertise in this regard.

PREFACE

This book is a collection of guidelines for Long-Range Planning adapted specifically to local churches, written from the personal experience and involvement of a lay leader and his pastor. It utilizes the techniques of planning from the corporate world, such as careful organization, purposeful activity, and decision-making. But, additionally, it has been applied to the problems and possibilities of church congregations, the pastors, and lay ministries.

The authors drew on their own experience to formulate the ideas and principles for action expounded in this publication. Dr. Richard M. Cromie was the Senior Minister of the Southminster Presbyterian Church in Mt. Lebanon, Pennsylvania from 1972 to 1983, a period in which the congregation experienced growth and prosperity. During that time Mr. Warren B. Davis served as a member of the Long-Range Planning Committee, mostly as chairman.

Because both the authors are Presbyterians, the nomenclature used here is largely that of the Reformed and Presbyterian tradition. There the ruling body is the Church Session, composed of ordained Elders, moderated by the Pastor, or the Senior Pastor. However, the principles enunciated here, we hope, will apply to any other church. We believe that the reader will be better able to interpret Presbyterian nomenclature according to his/her own concepts and structures, rather than the authors trying to visualize and translate the terms to a myriad of other systems of government.

This book is intended to be a handbook: a How-To-Do-It manual, which delineates a method of Long-Range Planning and then suggests areas of particular concerns and possible actions. Last, but not least, it includes a Scriptural argument for the use of the method suggested as being compatible with the teachings of Jesus Christ.

The authors present it in the hope that, since it grew out of a successful pattern in one congregation, it could become a help to others, as we struggle to be and become the Church of Jesus Christ.

CONTENTS

INTRODUCTION

All across the nation we can imagine pastors asking, "Who has time to spend on Long-Range Planning?" Rushing to get things done in the busy hum of ministerial matters, we hear them saying, "There is no time left for what we want to do already." Planning committee meetings mean more and more time, talk and more talk, dreams and more dreams, all accomplishing next to nothing. Following a recent seminar address on the need to plan, one minister told us, "I am a Man of Action!" So he was, we guess, at least he shuffled his feet and papers around a lot.

Well, the authors of this book are men of action, too. We come to bear personal witness to the need for action, born out of our concern for the Church of Jesus Christ in all of its locations, and out of the eleven years we worked together in a large, dynamic Presbyterian Parish near Pittsburgh, Pennsylvania, where "action" was the watchword of all we tried to do. "Action" *is* the goal.

But, we believe in intentional and productive "action", arising out of a special kind of long-range thinking and planning, the kind of activity which is directed to chosen ends and goals. Otherwise there comes a helter-skelter, hurry-it-up, rush around, spin-the-wheels kind of frenzy which is exhausting, and which, in the end, simply joins hands with too many weak and sorry failures of our fast moving world. The result, once more, is fragmentation.

1

* * *

Good churches do not arise by accident, neither do "good" lives, or "good" vocabularies, or "good" muscles, or "good" marriages. When "goodness" is seen, however you care to define it, you can be sure that it came from planned and purposeful activity. When you see "goodness" in a congregation, you can be sure that it also had been charted by someone who had the authority to choose for the entire congregation, and having chosen, chose to act.

Such goodness is more apparent, to be sure, when you personalize it. The goodness of my life is related to how carefully I plan my future days and decades, or even prior to the present, how my parents and others planned it for me. My health, my work, my success is more than coincidence. Actions have consequences. Although many surprises and disappointments come willy-nilly all along the way, mostly, as Robert Browning once observed, life gives us back what we ask for. We think the Bible says that too, especially the New Testament and the teaching of our Lord, both to our individual Christian lives and to congregations.

* * *

. The proper task of this book begins with the question of whether Long-Range Planning is compatible with the teachings of Jesus. With this initial discussion, we are saying how much the Bible means to us, and how ardently we believe that the New Testament teaches us to be well-planned and well-prepared. To be sure, there are many other items on the agendas of successful people and prospering churches, but one sure truth is that the community of God's people normally blossoms and flourishes in accordance with the way it seeks to plan its future. We get what we ask for. We find what we seek. We select the door, knock, and it is opened.

Of course, there is, and must always be, room for the "Surprises of God". No planning committee should ever pretend to usurp the power of the Holy Spirit to guide His people, or even to direct that Power (as if they could). Planning is no panacea. We have not joined hands with those who preach that good Long-Range Planning will usher in the Kingdom of God in the next five years, or so. We have been around too long to expect easy answers. The bottom line of this little book is, however, that we have seen this type of planning succeed in practice for almost a dozen years. In one particular congregation, where the results can be measured, we felt and feel the power of this message.

When you notice that a congregation is succeeding in Evangelism, or in Singles' Ministry, or in Peace-making, or in Christian Education, or in Programs for the Elderly, or in Mission Outreach; or even if you just simply notice that the church building and grounds look attractive and well cared for, you can be sure that a conscious decision was made to sort through the myriad of possibilities and someone in the congregation selected the item you observed. After the selection then, someone with authority carried through on that decision. It is elementary, my dear Watson, but sure and final!

We are offering this guide for your use in hopes that it will spark an additional interest and provide some additional tools for making good use of Long-Range Planning in your local church. First, however, we must discuss some fundamentals in order to focus more closely on what the church is or should be planning for.

Chapter I

THE PLACE TO BEGIN:
LONG RANGE PLANNING IN
THE TEACHING OF JESUS

Since we basically believe that only those activities which are derived from the Scripture, in intent and practice, belong on a church's agenda, we begin by locating Long-Range Planning within the teachings of Jesus Christ. Many people we have encountered through the years have been doubtful whether such planning activity is a proper function for a Christian organization which lives by the Grace of God. So we will deal with that question first. Since one person's starting point is beyond the finish of another, this section will seem elementary to some, but to others it will be the essential turning point.

Some church leaders, we know, who do not consider Planning a proper procedure, talk about the spontaneity of following the guidance of the Spirit. After all, in the wilderness, God did provide a pillar of cloud by day and a pillar of fire by night. Further, the Bible continually cautions that we do not ever know what a day might bring forth, let alone a year. Five-year-plans then appear to be foreign to the purpose of the Bible.

After all, Abraham went down through the valley, not knowing whither he was going. The prophets and priests and people alike awaited the immediate presence of Yahweh to tell them what to do or say next. And, most ominous of all, it says later, that our Lord will return without notice, coming as a thief in the night. Some other passages seem to indicate that Jesus himself had no need for planning, and that he cautioned his disciples not to wed themselves to their own ideas of the present generation, or to devise their "plans" for the future.

We read:

> ... *they will lay their hands upon you and persecute you ... and you will be brought before kings and governors for my name's sake. ... Settle it therefore in your minds, not to meditate beforehand how to answer; for I will give you a mouth and wisdom, which none of your adversaries will be able to withstand or contradict.*

> *Luke 21*

> *"I go to prepare a place for you. And when I go and prepare a place for you, I will come again and will take you to myself, that where I am you may be also. And you know the way where I am going." Thomas said to him, "Lord, we do not know where you are going; how can we know the way?" Jesus said to him, "I am the way, and the truth, and the life; no one comes to the Father, but by me. If you had known me, you would have known my Father also; henceforth you know him and have seen him".*

> *John 14*

Here, Jesus is urging the disciples to plan for a very different and difficult future which they cannot know in detail. Until He comes again, it seems to say, they will be able to manage on their own. We are inclined to go further, and to look on this as a charge to all

Christians to help the church to deal with an uncertain future in an effective way.

In his teaching from the Sermon on the Mount, Jesus also says:

> *Therefore I tell you, do not be anxious about your life, what you shall eat or what you shall drink, nor about your body, what you put on. . . . But seek first his kingdom and his righteousness, and all these things shall be yours as well. Therefore do not be anxious about tomorrow, for tomorrow will be anxious for itself. Let the day's own troubles be sufficient for the day.*
>
> *Matthew 6*

There are enough worries for today, that is for sure. Whirling around this spinning planet are monumental burdens like: Nuclear Armaments, Poverty, Human Rights, Race Relations, Hunger, Loneliness, etc. etc. Within each community, home, and person there are endless more, literally far too numerous to mention. They do cause us to be anxious today, and they should.

Now, the authors do not pretend to be New Testament scholars or professional exegetes, but the word which Jesus uses which is translated "anxious", is the key to understanding what we think he means. The original word in the Greek New Testament is a word which can be translated in a variety of ways. We use the Revised Standard Version here. The King James Bible says, "Take no thought for tomorrow". Wycliff translated it "be not busy with your life". The Good News Bible adds, "This is why I tell you, do not be worried about the food and drink you need".

In all cases, it does not seem that the attempt to plan a fruitful life is being condemned. Fruitless worry over incidentals is the concern. God cares for His children, and it says, He will provide food and raiment as needed. The previous warning from Jesus that we must not store up our treasures in larger and larger barns, only to lose them all in an instant, is near the heart of this passage also. He is urging us to be more carefree, to work less on our good works and to enjoy more of the good life. Being "anxious" is worrying, instead of doing something about the worry to improve the situation.

Good planning does not thrive well in "anxious" soil. Impatient people do not tend to do well on Long-Range Planning Committees (LRPC). In our experience we would often spend two hours in a meeting discussing matters like "the future of the world", or what it means to be a "Presbyterian", or "what will happen to the church when the baby-boom comes of age". Planning consists of being prepared, as Christ also commands, prepared to meet our Maker and with the Keys to the Kingdom in hand, to show Him what we have done, and tried to do, with the talents we have received. It takes patience, too.

From the beginning the Bible teaches us that God has a plan for His world. The universe was created with a purpose, for a purpose. The God of the Bible, as we have so often learned, is a God who ACTS, who moves us on to the future, who is concerned with what happens here and now, between the times, but the times which we are in-between are very long indeed.

What is more, Christ has a plan for His people, the Church. Seeds are planted in good soil, He taught, and then they grow. We are commanded to use our talent, not to bury it in the ground. Seeds go in the ground, not talent. We, as the people of the church, are the custodians of all that God intended from the day the earth was made. We need to be open to His guidance. We need to be ready for His coming. But we need also to move ourselves forward, bringing our best plans and purposes, to prepare ourselves and our children to expand the WITNESS of the Church we love and serve.

Chapter II
WHICH WAY SHALL WE GO?

The Planning process often begins with the question of what kind of congregation the pastor and the people wish to be. We advise all churches to be prepared for movement, especially at the point of each new passage in their corporate life: say, with the arrival of a new pastor, or with significant changes in the surrounding community, or with new challenges from the Church Hierarchy, whether it be the Bishop, the General Assembly, the General Conference etc. When these times come, the local outpost of Christ's reconciling work is in an ideal position to respond and rediscover its purpose.

The "passage" need not be earth-shattering. It could come when concerned members (or even the pastor) notice a decline in enthusiasm or attendance, or when someone begins to ask, "What are we going to do about . . . ? How are we going to overcome the problem, or to capitalize on the newness offered?" There the planning process quietly begins. The congregation is then asking: "What kind of a church do we want to be, in this situation? What issues should we address? What age-group seems to need our primary effort? What community problem is most urgent?" Etc. Etc.

The authors of this volume have discovered that one congregation cannot do everything, nor should it try. In trying to accomplish "everything", churches tend to end up accomplishing "nothing". For a little time at Southminster we had a "Worship Plus One" program for membership involvement. We concluded that worship was a must for each Christian. Every congregation should major its every effort to make the worship service a time of grace and the grandeur of God's presence. Without the strongest possible central service, it is unlikely that much more will happen. The "Plus-one" was then added. The "One" is imperative, i.e. one as opposed to "many". Otherwise you have a few members doing ten things each. One extra involvement beyond worship attendance was requested of each and every member. Realistically it often could not happen, but it was always our goal.

Broadened to congregational planning, we recommend that one, and only one, additional emphasis be made at a time. Large churches with larger staffs can often develop an expertise in many areas, but for the most part, in the beginning stages of our planning process, we would do well to add ONE new direction, at least only one at a time. Otherwise energy will be drained into dozens of areas and ideas, frustration will result, and the plans will literally go down the drain. So, we say:

A. Choose a Single Direction

As, Alice in her Wonderland, inquired one day of the Cheshire Cat how she could get out of there. To which he replied, "It depends where you want to go". Alice answered that she didn't really care; she simply wanted out. And then the prophetic reply of the Cheshire Cat, "It does not really matter then which way you go, does it?" If you do not know where you want to go, it is unlikely you will ever get there, and, we always add, if you do get there, you will not know where you are. In choosing a direction, there are some items we found to be essential:

(1) First, you must try to become the congregation which God requires you to be. Otherwise you might succeed, but ultimately you will fail. If you believe in a "Particular Purpose" for churches, as for nations and individuals, *i.e.,* if you believe congregations come upon the scene not when they choose, but when the Lord has need of them, then the search for theological power and purpose is the place to begin. Your goal is to find out what God's Purpose is. If you do not have a general agreement on what that purpose is, fear not, you have a wonderful agenda for your first six long-range planning meetings.

(2) Second, after you agree on a 'purpose' you should investigate the needs around you. A congregation in South Florida finds different problems and possibilities from a congregation in Western Pennsylvania. Small towns are not large towns. College communities are not downtown areas. New York is not San Francisco. London is not Aberdeen. Sagamore is not Atwood. The Purpose of God lies at the heart of each and all, but that power and purpose is mediated in a variety of different ways.

A church needs to consult with others in the immediate world around it. It needs to tie into community planning, councils and other available resources. It needs to walk around the neighborhood, to keep ears and eyes and mind open to all that is there, actually and potentially. When Dr. Schuller suggested at his Pastor's Conference, that we must "Find a need and fill it", he gave a great piece of advice. We will offer some examples later which document how one congregation tried to identify the needs of our area, but the important item here is that your church must set out to discover what ministries are essential and possible in the specific soil in which the Lord has planted you.

(3) The third and final suggestion in finding "The Place To Begin" is to analyze the resources which are available to you, especially within your untapped membership. We sometimes think the second most important talent for clergymen and clergywomen should be "the talent to uncover talent", to hitch up the appropriate power to pull the potential wagons which will move the Church of Christ ahead. The skill of identifying what jobs there are to do, and who is there to do them, is an area in which too few excel—partly we agree, because it is difficult to fathom, but partly the failure to make the match arises out of neglect. That makes it all the more important that your Long-Range Planning group work hard at discovering the array of talent available within your congregation

and community. A survey at the highest professional point you can afford will help, but initially it can be accomplished when sensitive thoughtful Christians begin to "look around".

God's purpose, your possibilities, and "people power" are the three-step place to begin before you can proceed with actual Long-Range Planning.

* * *

God does have a plan and purpose for His world. Before the foundations of the earth were ever laid, before the *terra firma* began to spin off around the Lazy Old Sun, the Lord God had predetermined what it all would be, and become. He had set the boundaries beyond which we will never go. There are nuances of Predestination here, an all too Presbyterian flavor for some, but we are projecting in a far broader theological context than our denominational origin might indicate. Between the times, with Eden gone and Armageddon far away (as far as we know), we are called to be the custodians of God's Good Earth, to be the caretakers to the East of Eden, as it were, and while, as they say in Florida, when the boat is drawing water, "We must pray toward Heaven . . . still, we must row toward shore".

We live in two worlds: the coming one, given in Promise and assured by God, the other, in the here and now. One foot on land, the Psalmist says, the other in the sea. When it comes to planning, "to be *in* and not *of* the world" means we must live in those two worlds at once: one here and one coming.

Depending upon the Grace of God to guide and guard our destinies, we still must use all the skills we have to plan the journey He has commanded us to take.

Chapter III
TO DEFINE THE TASK

How 'long' is Long-Range Planning? How far away should a long-range committee try to look? There are, and have been, many different answers in the years since congregations began to use Planning as a tool of ministry. Borrowing from the international political scene, some preach a "Five Year Plan". We are old enough to remember when the Soviet Union announced its first Five Year Plan, then another, and another. Others have thought in terms of a Ten Year Plan, or even longer, depending on the urgency involved. The definition of the ideal time is flexible.

Yet, when we experienced the changes of our time, and with Future Shock forever upon us, the authors here were led to a far more modest goal. We will later mention a possible Plan of Action, which will cover a longer period of time, but we came to define "Long-Range Planning" as *the attempt to look beyond the current year.* The presently active church officers and members will be immersed (we hope) in their present tasks and urgent committee assignments. Anything beyond what they are presently doing then, belongs in our definition of "Long-Range". A single year's program is sufficient for the year, whether it be in budget development, the stewardship of financial pledges, the program for next summer's vacation church school, the leaking roof, even next Sunday's sermon and church school classes. All that, and more, belong to the immediate short range. The long-range interest begins where the short range plans end.

It seems important to remind ourselves that each and every church has a long-range plan of some kind. At one extreme it may consist simply of a conviction on the part of some of the members or the minister that, "Someday we should find the funds to build a youth lounge"; or "Sometime we will have to find a way to repair the organ, fix the roof, or replace the concrete in the pavement at the corner". A potential plan is always there, however dormant.

At the other extreme, the governing body of the parish can begin to take a long, hard and reasoned look at its direction. If it does, it might then go on to appoint several qualified members to a formal Long-Range Planning Committee, (LRPC) which will then be assigned the task of exploring systematically the surrounding environment, the things somebody has been wishing for some time, and to bring some order to the possibilities. It then must visualize the problems which might arise, and suggest methods of conducting the advance that will minimize the difficulties, and maximize the opportunities to get underway with the future work of the Kingdom. The authors obviously believe that the closer a church comes to the second of these two extremes, the better chance it will have to survive and expand its ability to spread the Gospel.

The function of Long-Range Planning in a congregation is not greatly different from that of strategic planning in a corporation. The intent in both cases is (a) to estimate what the future environment will be like, including an investigation of the uncertainty of the future, (b) to visualize the problems that will arise from that uncertain future, and (c) to estimate what actions are needed, and when they will be needed to accomplish the principal objectives of the organization. Obviously the kind of environment that most affects a local church is not precisely that which affects a corporation. The objectives of churches and corporations are quite different. Nevertheless we have found many basic principles of planning are common to both. If you can enlist the support of a member with Corporate Planning experience, you will have an able ally indeed. Many of the Southminister Committee members, including James I. Mosley, who was a competent and caring chairman for quite a few years, had tremendous practical training through their daily employment.

Chapter IV

HOW TO ORGANIZE YOUR EFFORTS: PROPERTY—PROGRAM—PEOPLE

In this short, alliterative phrase: Property, Program, People; planners and the pastor will find a memorable little secret opening through which to keep their thoughts in order.

A. Property

The church facilities are not the most important element of effective ministry, not by a long shot. Many effective communities of God's People have no meeting place at all. The earliest church met in homes, or darkened alley-ways. Our own church began in a school. But, *Property* is the easiest place to begin. Trying to fashion the needs of program and people presents more complex and illusive choices. These needs can be handled in time, but Property begins the focus since it gives the Congregation a particular "habitation and a name". Everyone who attends, or wants to, can see what is going on.

If the pastor and the people believe that the church properties belong to God, and, that literally, as the Old Testament suggests, the Sanctuary is the Dwelling Place of the Lord, then we need to treat the Church Property accordingly. Haggai asks in the Old Testament if it is fair for the people to dwell in their own paneled houses, while the Temple lies in ruin. The times were different then, of course. But Haggai's image lingers on. We have other missions to accomplish, other chores to challenge, and other things to do. But an important part of the planning process is to ensure that our location of Christ's Kingdom be committed to the preservation and improvement of the building and its grounds. In the event that your parish, as ours, holds title to several different properties, in that case, they all belong to God.

This whole question is related to a stewardship of natural resourses and our attempts to preserve the beauty of the earth. Without that beginning, all else can fail. Such commitment goes far beyond the worship area. For practical and popular reasons, we add, concentration on the condition of the church facilities is a sure-fire way to enlist support of practical-minded people, really not as political as the sentence might sound. In order to do the work of ministry and mission successfully, we need to provide a means of accomplishment for the people who are involved. Each and everyone can see the surroundings, and even the dullest among us can enjoy the result of proper care and concern for the property. One man we know actually joined our church and contributed enormously just after we planted a spring garden at our most conspicuous corner!

But further to our purposes, we found that we were working against ourselves at Southminster in an antiquated office area. Our Christian Education and "Office" building, as many others of its vintage, was constructed in the day when a "church staff" normally begged, borrowed, or "stole" from other areas to house the growing staff of Assistant Ministers, Christian Education Directors, machine rooms, secretarial space, room for volunteers, etc. etc.

We did not feel the need to compete with Wall Street Suites (of which we were accused), or with the Corporate Executive floors in Pittsburgh's finest companies (one of which was done over with exquisite oriental taste). But, we did discover the need for a pleasant place to house our employees. We needed additional space for additional clergy and efficient filing systems for our church information. We needed comfortable temperature, a conference room, a lunchroom for the office employees, etc., etc. That all sounds elementary, but we had to "sell" the idea to those who felt the purpose of the church was to give all of its money away to missions, or to evangelize the neighborhood. Those were the days of "no-church churches". In the end, we changed the context of our work. We altered what people thought about what a church could be. It also took a major renovation, and a costly one at that, which stretched from the worship area to educational space, to good music rehearsal rooms, to etc. etc. And, one day, even our fiercest critic came by to say: "Yes, How lovely is Thy Dwelling Place, O Lord".

Similarly with our youth area, in working with the committee chairmen and the leaders of the teenagers themselves, we developed a plan for what was needed in the youth area. It took four or five years to do it all (in fact, we never got it entirely done), but step by step, we cleared an area that was out of the way, but suitable. Through our Reverend Jack Lolla, we invited a youthful architect to work with the young people themselves to propose a whole new meeting area. Eventually the floors (thanks to Jim Morgan), ceilings, and walls were all carpeted (unusual but useful). Giant benches were placed all around the room and the ancient piano was even restored. In the end the new area accomplished its purpose: the young people loved to be there, and they came in droves to enjoy it.

* * *

For our music program we tried to do the same. If you want a large, important choir program, you need to provide large, important choir facilities. If you want rehearsals to go well, you must develop the appropriate space which is pleasant, accoustically sound, etc. If you want choir members of all ages to think well about themselves and what they do, you need to provide suitable (even scrumptious) places for robes, lockers, rehearsal chairs, attractive rooms, et al. Or as a friend of ours likes to say, "If you want to be first class, try to look as if you are". Margaret Mead once said, "Life belongs together". It all fits in a pattern; there are no missing pieces to the puzzle. That is true in church work, too.

* * *

We do not present a panacea, to be sure, but it took us a long, long time to learn how important property is. (You need to remember that we began our work together back when the institutional life of the Christian Church was being challenged and threatened by the "New" Form of Christianity.) The church building, and grounds around it, we came to believe, still told outsiders what we thought and felt about ourselves. Appearance either does or does not appeal to the "sense of beauty". If you can tell what a person thinks about himself by how he or she looks, so can you gather what an entire congregation feels and thinks about itself by how completely it dresses up or by the "image" it presents to the outside world. Tacky, beat-up old chairs, walls, halls, meeting rooms, gardens, sign boards, etc. lead visitors, as well as non-committed members, to believe the same about every thing else. If it is *The House of God,* help to make it look as if it qualifies.

* * *

B. Program

"Program" is the name we use to describe the various activities of the local congregation. The goal of Program is to provide activities which *will help all the people to grow in body, mind, and soul,* and to help them to have fun and good Christian fellowship in the process. There is a time to change the world. There is a time to weep about the sufferings of God's children. There is a time for many other things. But, there is also a time to laugh, a time to be together, a time to gather the strength we need to do all of those other "times".

We encourage you to make Planning fun. Our Long-Range Planning meetings were hilarious at times. We normally came away exhilarated, bounding with joy over all the things we planned to do, scheming little ways to motivate the folk who sat upon their hands and stubbornly resisted change. The "creative foot-draggers" were not normally an object of our abuse, but we smiled at how we could end-run the objections of the masses.

* * *

To succeed in Program, we used simple schemes. With pencil and paper in hand, we made some arbitrary divisions of what we could call "Program". Our way was to list activities divided up by the ages of the members and their families. For example, on one sheet of paper we wrote "Age one to six". (If the family had such a child, whatever the age of the parents, they belonged.) We next wrote down every single program which our congregation provided for preschoolers. Then, say grades one to six, then Junior High, then Senior High, then young adults, then young families, then the middle-aged, then the retired, then shut-ins, etc. We did not fail to include Men and Women's ministries, or Singles. We wrote down everything which we provided for each and every group, *ad infinitum*.

Your searching will surprise you, we think, by how many things are currently being done for these age groups and interests. For example, everyone of every age is provided for in worship. Each and everyone is entitled to pastoral care. Each and everyone receives the newsletters and the bulletin. Every meeting is a potential "small group" ministry. Everyone is permitted to call upon the church for help. We suggest a beginning survey by your committee: "What do we actually offer for each and every age group?"

* * *

When this task is finished, we suggest that next you select the areas in the congregation and community where the needs seem to be the greatest, often quite illusive and difficult, but a worthwhile process. In order to complete it, we decided to attack a particular phase of program each and every year. For example, we asked everyone we could think of in our entire church: the Staff, our Session, our Trustees, our Deacons, the Women's Groups, Youth etc., all of them and more to focus for one year on the "The Special Project" of the year. One time it was "The Family". Another time it was "The Elderly". Another time it was "The Singles". Whatever project we chose, the Trustees were charged to budget for the concern. The Session had each committee respond to the challenge, etc. For example, in the "Family Year", the Senior Highs were encouraged to do inter-generational programs. The Session authorized a special series on family development. At every staff meeting the agenda included what staff was doing for the Christian "Family". A special Task Force Committee systematized the whole program. Out of that whole procedure, there grew the now most successful "Family Center", a comprehensive program which continues to grow with gusto as it ministers, with Grace, to a wide variety of "Family" needs. Similar efforts were made for Singles Ministry, for Senior Citizens, for Youth, for Young Couples, etc. etc.

It is necessary, of course, to plan for programs of outreach, also. Mission involvement on the local, national or world wide levels, will always be an essential part of the program of the community of Christ's people. It will be obvious to say that certain gatherings of God's Children will make certain assumptions in that regard. Those assumptions must be honored. Yet, change is the order of God's day. A particular people need not continue an historic emphasis, just because it is historic. A great past is great, but you cannot live on a great past. God always calls us forward.

* * *

In our case at Southminster we had a long and illustrious history as a concerned congregation. There was, and is, great diversity of the membership in what some members believed and practiced and others did not. (By the way, it was not so diverse as we assumed. A survey of ideas and attitudes prepared by Mr. Davis of all of our officers revealed a remarkable uniformity!) But as we went along, the tension was terrific. Muscleheads as well as muscles grow in tension. The "exercise" often hurts, but without it nothing happens at all. After all, pain is part of growing.

The important function of the Church Planner is to help the congregation decide which way to go, by identifying as many as possible of the needs and possible directions mentioned above. Our concerns led us, for example, to a strong Peacemaking commitment, long heralded by many but re-issued when the General Assembly of our Denomination made it a national priority, an action by the way which our Long-Range Planning Committee called to the attention of the Session committee. From that opening came a still-vital commitment to the priority of Peace.

We also were led along the way to a massive church-wide commitment to Hunger Relief, especially in the local area, then to a resettlement of refugees, to ecumenical issues, and to countless other church and community commitments. The appropriate committees led the way. New task forces were almost always developed for the larger issues; but we must say that almost each and every new commitment arose out of the basic question of the kind of church we desired to be. Wherever the idea came from, it seems that it was nourished (or nullified) in Long-Range discussions.

The Program helps to organize activity, to select priorities, and to focus, one step at a time, on getting the job accomplished. We suppose there is no better description on what Long-Range Planning is, or should be, than to define the task, and then accomplish it! AMEN.

* * *

C. People

Without "People" nothing at all in the church would happen. We divide "people ministries" into two parts: The Church Professional Staff, and The Laity. We begin with staff: not because the ministers and other professionals are more important, but that without them the task of planning in the church in next to impossible. If you do not have the right staff, the task of Long-Range Planning, as well as everything else you seek to do, will be exceedingly difficult, and no doubt result in dead-end roads. We believe in the action of the laity out of our prior belief in the priesthood of all believers, but, if the minister and staff do not care about planning, the job we describe will never be completed. If some key officers refuse to open up their vision, the journey is an infinitely larger task. If the Senior Minister opposes it, it will be finished.

By "Staff" we mean the people who work regularly at the church. That includes clergy, secretaries, custodians, and others. It includes also part-time people too. We adopted a technique, largely in use all across the land, of employing part-time people for specific tasks. For instance, a young woman who worked twenty hours a week tried to spearhead our Singles' Ministry. The Senior Citizen's program has had two supremely qualified part-time leaders. The Family Center began with one part-time person and now has another. Both were/are excellent.

* * *

We have noticed a reluctance of church people to make changes in staff members, thereby protecting legacies of servanthood far beyond the time when productive work is accomplished. Because these souls have always been involved, it seems to many to be cruel to move them on. We venture to say that it could be worse to allow them to continue. If your custodian, for example, is not equipped to take care of the church grounds and property properly, then we suggest that you supervise his work, and call the deficiencies to his attention. Next set some specific goals. And, if the goals are not met at all, issue a first and final reminder. Then, when all else has failed, as it no doubt will, if you have gone this far, we suggest that you find the courage to terminate the employment. We have found through the years that problems do not go away unless someone with courage (Christian courage we might add) begins to solve the problem, not prolong it.

* * *

To plan a church staff is to analyze the needs of the church and to find the Christian people who can fill these needs. The alternative is to accede to those who are there. If you try to be nice all day long, if you try to be gentle, meek, and mild, you will find the good people smiling at you as you pass, but everything will remain the same. You need to have good staff, well chosen and well trained, to accomplish the tasks of the current Christian Church. Do not let your heart rule your head. Or, as Harry Truman used to say, "If you see what you have to do, next you ought to do it!"

On the other hand, it is imperative to say that a good staff does not arrive by accident either. The selection process for each and every paid employee must be done with great care and without unbearable compromise. Too many times we see someone's brother or son or sister-in-law given the job. Or we have heard that a good Christian woman has just lost her job before she is offered the recently opened Church secretary's position. After all, the Elder said, we have "to take care of our own". That we do, but it takes enormous undoing to remove the Elder's brother from the work which is not being done, six months or six years later. We finally had our Session pass a near-absolute rule that church members were not eligible for employment. No doubt too arbitrary for some, but it helped us, that is for sure.

The time and endless energy required in the search for a suitable staff cannot be over-emphasized. We came to believe that a large part of it has to do with our ability and willingness to pay suitable wages and other benefits. The local church often is the last to realize that employees have rights to good wages, good working conditions, good spaces, and, as many benefits as the employing congregation can afford to manage.

* * *

We add finally, with our bias to be sure, that no Pastor-Search committee should ever fail to ask the potential new pastor and preacher: "What do you think about Long-Range Planning in the church?"

The peculiar needs of the kind of church staff you will need might vary. But, the principles elaborated here will remain forever the same.

* * *

A second part of *"People"* is the Laity. Simply said: you need the right people to do the right job, or the job will not be done. Part of the Pastor's role is to see that the laity are selected and trained to do their work. If your congregation does not have a significant lay training program, then you must surely start one. No church will ever rise above the level of its officers. It will rise only in proportion to the way in which the leaders understand the purposes which lie behind the commitment of Christ to the local institution. Theological and Biblical training are as essential to the new leaders as leadership skills might ever be. Beyond the original purpose, your leaders will need the skills to be able to do their chosen work. Both go hand in hand. Frustrations will ensue unless the pastor and the council find ways to train and accomplish their tasks. Then, so that satisfaction will be assured, a system for accountability must be developed. We all need to know how we are doing, including the people of the church.

This means that the minister must be free to delegate significant decision-making processes to the various laity and their created committees of the church. He/she has plenty to do in preaching, teaching, and pastoring. In our view, the Pastor (or Senior Pastor) is the Captain of the ship. But, having once identified the goals for lay involvement, and having provided proper training so that the laity can do their proper work, the pastor then must step aside and watch with wonder as God's people accomplish it, with gusto and with grace. To suggest a final little secret, the pastor still can take the credit . . . because no one will believe that laity could accomplish all that by themselves. (Ha, Ha, Ha, Ha, Ha!)

Chapter V

HOW TO FORM THE COMMITTEE

The most crucial participant in a Long-Range Planning effort is the Pastor, or in multiple staff situations, the Senior Pastor! If he (or she) does not participate, we repeat, there is little chance that a Long-Range Planning Committee will accomplish anything worthwhile. The pastor must attend enough meetings, and participate in enough discussions, so that the committee (and particularly the chairman) is in tune with the pastoral leader's ambitions and goals for the congregation. If the majority of the committee disagrees with the Senior Minister's outlook on any important subject, then that subject should be discussed, until some kind of preliminary or compromise agreement has been reached. Ideally, the committee should be an extension and expansion of the minister's thinking on matters which affect the future of the church. If wise, the minister will listen for the voice of God in the voice of the committee. One can be led as well as lead. Amen.

It is dangerous we realize to place the clergyperson in so elevated a significant posture as herein stated. Our estimate could backfire and appeal to the prima donna aspect, which hides inside each (and we would say 'every') successful pastor. It also means that concerned laity can be thwarted without ministerial support. We take the risk, however, because we have found it to be true. Unless the Pastor, or Head Pastor, is on the side of Long-Range Planning, however docile is his reluctance, the plans will *never* be accomplished!

* * *

The chairman of the commitee (male or female) should be a person with considerable imagination. He/she should have an innate tendency to study problems rather than solve them. He/she should have a willingness to delegate part of a problem to other people. He/she should have some kind of predisposition, or some experience in Planning. And he/she should have some ability to control a meeting to keep it from rambling out of control. (It also helps tremendously if he/she shares the view of the clergyperson in charge.)

The most likely professional area for finding these characteristics is the Staff of a large company. But that is not the only place. Many housewives can become the greatest planners in the world. They after all deal in looking ahead. We urge you to select the committee carefully. The appointment of a "line" business executive as chairman of the (LRPC) committee is likely to fail. Those who deal with the day-in, day-out management of a company, are trained to look at the available facts, and to make quick immediate decisions. These types do not do well on Long-Range matters.

Many of the commissions or committees of a congregation need another style of leadership. Immediate action is a *sine qua non* of many action oriented tasks.

Quick decisions are not needed in Long-Range Planning. Many successful "salesmen" normally are not good at "planning". Some are, we have found, but the primary task of a salesman is to sell. They do wonderfully in stewardship drives. The primary task of a Long-Range Planner is to Plan—and to think, the "Chief Glory" of us all.

* * *

You will need a chairman who has strong opinions, but who is skilled at devising good group activity, and a "shared" approach to the shared problem. He (or she) should be prepared to be patient. The leader must have the additional brain-power to dream dreams and see visions (not literally we hope). But, the chairman must also be careful in the endless search for detail. Often a set of carefully gathered historical figures can be the key which unlocks the puzzle before the committee's eyes. The chairman must be willing to take the necessary time, however long it takes. He must be loyal to his church and loyal to the pastor and to the common goals in Christ which lie before us all.

So much more could be said, but the point being made is that the pastor should not direct the Long-Range Planning Committee. A lay person should. The kinds of skills and talents the potential chairman has, will largely determine how effective the process will become.

The other members of the Long-Range Planning Committee (we recommend a group no larger than nine) should represent a broad cross-section of the membership of the church. If you have Deacons, Trustees and/or other Official Boards, try to make sure that all Boards are represented; women and youth should be represented as well. People with differing outlooks are needed also, but all of them should have that irreplaceable quality of imagination and a willingness to discuss the problems with an ever open mind. A commitment to the unity and over-all good of the church is essential. Differences of opinion should be encouraged, and a wide range of abilities and experiences will be helpful to the committee's assignment.

* * *

The members of our "Session" in our tradition are elected for a three year term. The tenure of members on commissions and committees in our tradition is often the same length of time. The tour of duty of the chairman of a commission normally, in our system, is often for only one year. A short term keeps such offices from being unduly burdensome to a lay person, and also insures "new life" in the forever expanding leadership of the church.

Membership on a Long-Range Planning Committee, however, should not be for a short, finite term, unless mandated by unforeseen reasons. It is not practical to appoint a member of this committee for the duration of all-time (to be sure). However, members of the LRPC should be chosen and encouraged to stay on the committee until circumstances make it impractical for them to remain, at which time a member can surely resign, and a new member be appointed. We tried to add one member each year.

Chapter VI

WHAT THE COMMITTEE SHOULD DO

The primary functions of a Long-Range Planning Committee are to visualize where the policies of a congregation might be leading it in the foreseeable future years, then to help the principal officers of the church visualize the predictable aspects of the future, and finally to persuade the officers to take into account the more-or-less predictable long-term future of the church.

In order to accomplish this, the LRPC must be in close, continuous communication with the chairman (or chairpersons, if you prefer) of all commissions (as we call them) and/or committees of the governing body. One way of doing this is to appoint a member of the LRPC as a Contact Person for each commission and/or committee. The Contact People could then speak with the chairman of the various groups at least once per month—and, we found, should attend at least one or two of the committee meetings during the year. Some part of each LRPC meeting also should be devoted to the various reports from the Contact Persons on the various committees. Our LRPC always asked committee chairmen to agenda "Long-Range" on the docket of each and every meeting—each and every meeting!

* * *

Occasionally, we discovered matters arise which do not fit in the regular committee structure of even the best organized congregation. In such cases, the LRPC should decide whether an *ad hoc* task force is needed to deal with the particular matter at hand. Or, as we occasionally did in our process at Southminister, we determined that these special matters could be retained and handled by the LRPC itself. Most items and projects originating in the Long-Range Committee are and should be referred to the appropriate committee assigned to the task. But if the LRPC defines the peculiar aspects of the problem, and then assigns the officers of the particular church ruling body to appoint an *ad hoc* task group, the continuity of action is insured. (Provided such a procedure is prescribed by the constitution of the particular body involved.) If the LRPC takes on more than just an occasional extraneous task, it will soon be bogged down with details and particular programs, and it will fail to carry out its primary task and the mission of moving the congregation to the future.

* * *

We have found that the study of what a Long-Range Planning Committee should *not* do, can be as important as what the LRPC should do. It should *never* become a "Short-Term Planning Committee". If the Session (or Council) of a congregation should happen to have some very argumentative people on it, so that meetings tend to turn into long, futile debates and useless harangues, please do *not* try to solve the problem by turning a LRPC into a cabinet which might consider all the church's unsolved problems, and which might try to reach solutions independently from the Session. If the LRPC is working smoothly, and the ruling body is not, the temptation to create a kind of "Kitchen Cabinet" is very great indeed. However, such procedure is a contravention of the Rules of Order necessary to be the church of your choice. The activities of a LRPC must be subject to the discipline of the denominational ruling body. The committees (or commissions) of that body must make short-term plans and then approve of any long-term plans which might be made. Otherwise pandemonium ensues. It is largely a matter of Theological commitment (we say with a capital "T") to the order of your particular form of government. We caution that you do not create a LRPC procedure which is intended to disorder the order of your organization. You will fail as a result, short and long term, too.

* * *

Some member of LRPC (preferably the chairman of the LRPC) should be an elected member of the Session (Council) of the church. We found that it is necessary that a LRPC member attend all meetings of the Session to keep the planning folk informed about critical issues, as well as in turn to present recommendations of LRPC to the Session, and to hear and carry to the various committees the comments (to say nothing of the 'actions') of the Ruling Body.

* * *

A LRPC with such broad functions as described herein can turn out to be the best organization to study some problems which are not strictly "Long-Range". We often found this to be true and helpful. For example, a study of a reorganization of the Session and Trustees of our Church, and all the various committees was such a problem. But, whatever they are, as long as such studies are done with knowledge and even tacit approval of the Session, they are proper functions of a LRPC because they do bear heavily on the day-to-day operation of the church. A short-range alteration, of course, is often necessary for the long-range destination!

* * *

We learned that there are usually three initial steps for each Long-Range Committee to take. They come in logical sequence in establishing the Planning System. A fourth must be added later: i.e. to devise a means of review for the first three. They are as follows:

I. "A PLANNING GUIDE", approved by the church governing board, which will set the goals of the congregation in the frame-work of the world and community around it, forecasting (as far as is possible) the kind of situations in which the church will have to live.

II. "A STATEMENT OF PURPOSE"

III. A series of measurable goals to be reached in so many years, which can then be consolidated into "A CHURCH PLAN" which will lay out the agreed purpose (or purposes) of the particular church to which you belong.

IV. Finally, you will then have to establish a SYSTEM OF REVIEW. The previous steps must always be revised and updated. Or, too soon the Long-Range Plans will be short range absurdities: outdated and useless.

The steps are:

I. The Planning Guide

First the compilation of a Planning Guide should be done by the Long-Range Planning Committee. It should obtain some estimates of the history and likely outlook for the factors which have affected and will affect the cultural environment in which your church exists, and will exist. A suggested list of subjects to be covered might be as follows. But we encourage your committee to "Think-Tank" the kinds of information which might help it. At least the following:

*A. National Trends

   1. U.S. population by age groups, sex, occupation, and social environment, with possible projections.

   2. Trends in Income, Employment, Economic Growth, Inflation rates, etc.

   3. Some measure of social trends, as far as you can see.

   4. Trends in church membership, church influence on society, and other national trends. You might be able to successfully

*Appendix A gives possible copy—   Page A-1.

buck national movements, but it is unlikely.

B. Your Own Community

1. Population trends: up or down, including a description of the proposed most likely changes.

2. Income and Employment Trends.

3. Church Membership Trends, et al.

C. Your Congregation

1. Membership: history with projection.

2. Attendance at Worship, past, present, and projected.

3. Attendance at Church School, Youth Activities, etc.

4. Revenues and Expenditures, including Benevolence.

5. Pledges—Number, Ranges and Potential.

6. Results of Special Fund Drives.

7. Emphasize "Potentials" to determine possible trends.

Note that it is not necessary or even desirable that LRPC members try to make accurate forecasts of these trends. You can use only "published forecasts" of easily obtained information in the public domain. We recommend you give only broad ranges of forecasts. For one thing they are more realistic than single-line forecasts; for another, that is all your people will need. The important goal is to select 'ranges' of outlooks. These and other factors your committee might think important will then be accepted as reasonable by the LRPC and eventually accepted by the Church Ruling Body. Specific forecasts of the trends of your own church are not necessary at this stage, not at all. Unless of course they are so obvious that a blind man could see.

Someone, however, should begin to compile an accurate history of your congregation. Often such historical material is difficult to find. We were blessed to be in a place where record-keeping was far above the average. A Saint named "Mutt" Rust had gathered all possible "pledge" information for the forty-six previous years. But, if you have no St. Mutt, go on to gather as much information as possible. Then, assemble it for future reference. (See Appendices for examples of what we were able to use for our projections.)

* * *

Since the individual parts of a Planning Guide can be prepared separately, we suggest that you delegate each part to a LRPC member (or some other) then review the assembled sections (wherever they are prepared) with the whole committee. A first draft of the assembled guide should be offered to each member of the church staff and (we found) each member of the Session. (Each congregation must determine *ex nihilo* what they will need to know.) But, be prepared then to allow several months for assigned persons to solicit comments and criticisms. When the predetermined time is up, we recommend that you publish the results and make it available to the members of the church.

Place the material in some convenient public place. (We chose the church library, off to the right of the left transcept.) We caution you that only a few energetic members other than the officers are ever likely to read it. But, do not be deterred (or disappointed) by a less than enthusiastic original response. We predict that this opening phase is likely to take at least one year. Good luck—if you can accomplish it sooner.

This is an important time. These original projections and proposals might seem to deter the development of a formal plan. Your most energetic officers will be reluctant to wait. But your task is to have the membership, staff, officers, and everybody else begin to think in Long-Range Plans and Patterns: a reorientation of vast proportions. The wheels of the Gods—to say nothing of Our God—grind slowly! Meanwhile, of course, the routine operation of the congregation is proceeding as per usual, we hope, and with the hint that someone "bright" is watching, even better.

* * *

II. A Statement of Purpose

Once you have drawn up a kind of *"Planning Guide"* for your location, the next step is to agree on a *Statement of Purpose*. In other words, ask the question: "What do we want our plan to accomplish". There is much value in this step, even if you are not going on to detail a formal plan for immediate action. The Statement of Purpose should be broad enough to include the diversity of your membership, but narrow enough to characterize the specific goals of your congregation. The Statement should begin with a simple declaratory statement declaring the particular cast, or character, of your congregation. There are a wide range of particular purposes for the various outposts of Christ's people.

For some the Introductory Statement might read, "Our purpose is to bring Jesus Christ to the non-believers in the world". Another might begin, "Our purpose is to become the reconciling presence of Christ in this alien world". Another, "Our purpose is to promote the Over-Seas mission of the church." Or, "Our basic purpose as a congregation is to bring Peace to the world around us." One church we know announced its basic purpose as the attempt to go out of existence and merge with the Methodists across the street. Whatever, the *Statement of Purpose* should lead with a *raison d'etre,* a basic reason for your existence as a congregation of Christ's people. If there is no especial purpose to define your presence, we frankly do not know what you should do.

The first draft of the *Statement* can be made by the Minister, in conjunction with the committee chairman, or it can be prepared by a competent "writer" in the group. Whatever, it should then be distributed to all of the LRPC members, and debated in a few of their meetings. When agreement has been relatively reached by the committee, we suggest that the Statement be submitted to all of the elected officers. Then it should be discussed in a formal Session meeting. Then, finally and formally adopted (hopefully) by the appropriate Ruling Body. It is desirable that the version adopted by the Session, as we mentioned, be made available then to all church members. We chose to print it in its entirety in a bulletin insert. We advise a consensus attitude by the committee before you proceed. No pride of authorship in its own work should prevent a willingness to allow the Session to make the final statement. Then the entire membership must be encouraged to comment. (Fear Not. We always find that ninety-five percent will be silent!)

Appendix B is an abbreviated example of a Statement of Purpose. This one was adopted by the Session of the Southminster Presbyterian Church several years ago. It is not placed here as an ideal statement, but as a starting idea of what one particular congregation determined was suitable at that time. Yours should reflect the outlook of *your* Senior Minister, *your* Session, *your* community and *your* commitment, at the especial time of its writing. It is not a static document. It should be reviewed annually (if possible) for its continued applicability. At Southminster, we reviewed it constantly and proposed an extensive revision every couple of years.

III. The Plan

After the Statement of Purpose, your congregation should be prepared to design a "Long-Range Plan". There are three arbitrary decisions which should be made before you begin this step.

1. Determine a Time Interval for Your Action.
2. Select the Critical Activities to be Covered.

3. Decide Who Will Initiate the Various Parts of the Plan.

There are no right or wrong or easy answers at this point, or at any other. But, we suggest that you do not delay in your determination by looking for the perfect Plan. If after an appropriate time you conclude that the initial Plan was defective, you can always correct the problem later on when you revise and review the Plan. You cannot design an effective Plan to help you proceed until these opening decisions have been made.

A Plan which does not look ahead at least five years could hardly be classified as a Long-Range Plan. This is not inconsistent with our earlier definition of long-range as "beyond one year". There we stated that "Long-Range Planning" begins with any Plans beyond the current year. That still is true. But real planning never ends. The Plan probably should include many things which can be started in the first couple of years, even if they cannot be completed. We all need *progress* to spark enthusiasm.

This "Plan" should attempt to deal with anticipated problems which will take much longer. It must seek to look four or five years ahead. If your Session and Minister see important projects that could possibly take Ten or even Twenty years to complete, then this "Plan" should be open-ended to allow for such extensions. One of the best long Long-Range Plans we know of is a Twenty-Five Year Plan where one congregation we know plans to give Twenty-Five Million

Dollars to Missions in the next Twenty-Five years. When in doubt, start with a shorter planning span. But Twenty-Five Million Dollars for Mission is worth a gander anyway. You can always increase or decrease at the next review, if necessary.

Selecting the "critical activities" which are to be covered in your Plan is probably the most difficult decision you will make. The assigned committee chairman and his/her committee of the Session should be asked to make the final decision for that especial area of activity. The authority is theirs. The church staff and the LRPC members, however, should not hesitate to make recommendations, even to prod reluctant church officers to proceed. An extended dialogue on this subject is critically important. In every church, there are some obvious needs to begin with: like membership development, or the amount of money needed to pay the institutional bills, or the need to support missions. We caution that a Plan based on broad generalities will in the end be less than useless. Your *Plan* must deal with the particular activities and figures you need to accomplish the purposes you have chosen. Otherwise it can be called "their" Plan, but never "yours" or "mine".

On the other hand, you must be careful not to weigh the Plan down with too many specific recommendations. If the Plan contains a huge mass of particular detail and seven hundred and one things to do, hardly anyone will read it, or adopt it, and, if they did, they could never accomplish it. The Church Session will not be able to allow the necessary time to understand the Plan, or to check its progress. The activities and goals should be stated in a way which can be measured, one at a time, all along the way. After that, a reporting procedure must be established, and records kept, so that the individual Church Ruling Body can determine whether the provisions of the Plan are being met. What a pity if no one cares enough to complain.

* * *

Although separate assigned committees must have final approval of those sections of the plan which relate to their area of activity, the committee does not necessarily initiate the Plan. It does not really matter who "initiates" the individual parts of the Plan, so long as all interested parties have a chance to be heard as the Plan develops. It is important, however, for someone to get the ball rolling in establishing specific responsibilities for initiating each part of the Plan. We found no better point of origin than an active and aggressive LRPC. Say a committee assigned to increase mission gifts to the poor was not functioning, we encouraged them to move. If not, we moved. The "we" is LRPC. Later we attach an example of the Plan of our congregation, adopted by the Session of our church. It is not an ideal Plan, except that it was ideal for us, at that time. Our committee thought that the activities listed were not all quantified as well as they should have been. We also agreed that some of the goals were too ambitious. But our committee added a peculiar flavor to the *potpourri* of the tasks and goals we wanted to accomplish. If our goals were too ambitious, we remind you that the Christian's reach must always exceed his grasp, or we will never know how far up and out we can go.

Some of our committee people felt that the Plan was too extensive, too difficult. The Senior Minister on the other hand often said the goals were not all as ambitious as they should have been. The total Session probably thought it contained too much detail, etc. etc. As against all this, The Plan compromised all of these diverse views and was finally approved by all responsible authorities. It was tailored to our congregation at a particular time. It will be different from yours, now. But it suggests the framework in which we all can work.

IV. Systematic Review

However successful you are in developing a Planning Guide, a Statement-of-Purpose, or a formal Plan, you must then set up a system to review the work of planning at regular intervals. One thing you can be sure of is that some (or even all) of your projections will be inaccurate. Moreover some, or all, of your workers will not work to highest expectations. If your Planning is to be of use to the congregation, you must detect the inaccuracies, find the foot-draggers, and correct both as time goes by. The Planning Guide should be reviewed and updated at an interval not to exceed five years. If the economic and social outlook changes significantly, it should be reviewed and updated in less time than that. (We found each two and a half year period was ideal.) The Statement of Purpose and The Plan should be reviewed by the Session yearly. If only to be sure that no picayune item was omitted, the review must take place.

Since the second year of a Plan becomes the next year's church budget and program (almost surely with some changes, but there nonetheless), it is desirable to add *another* year to the Plan each passing year. That way it will be a living, moving Plan. We recommend that the Ruling Body, the Session, devote one full meeting per year, perhaps a special meeting for that purpose only, to review the Plan, and hear reports and recommendations by the commission chairmen, and others who care.

The primary benefit of a Long-Range Plan is *not* to be accurate in its forecasts. To be "right" is a luxury the LRPC may forego. Its peculiar power comes in persuading church staff, officers, and the entire membership to take the Future into account in making decisions on current matters. Tomorrow is here as soon as today is over. As our title says, before you know it: *The Future Is Now!*

Chapter VII

THE PLAN IN ACTION

We have attached to this chapter one of the more recent "Plans for Action", which originated in the Long-Range Committee, was approved by the Church Session, and hopefully was carried out by the various committees and church staff members of Southminster. The process of trying to live up to this Plan was a marvelous experience for all of us. One of the most rewarding results of the Long-Range Planning Committee's work was participating as we proceeded to do what we determined to do.

The Long-Range Committee received permission from the Church Session to draft an original Plan of Action for each of the committees and commissions including the Board of Trustees, the Church Session itself, the Woman's Association, the Board of Deacons, etc.

The items listed in each particular portion of the Plan came from a variety of sources, partly from interviews with the staff, partly from interviews with current and past chairmen of the various committees, partly out of a "dream discussion" in one of our Long-Range Planning Committee meetings about what we dreamed our church could be, a process repeated at an officer training event, and partly we pray from the presence of God's Guiding Spirit.

* * *

Concurrent with the development of the Plan, the LRPC was observing the current yearly work of the various committees. We solicited input from our Presbyterian officials. We wrote to New York to see what they had to offer. We were blessed to have several seminary faculty members and other ordained clergy in our congregation who, with their families, assisted us. We employed a corporate planner and trainer to conduct an officer's retreat. The Senior Pastor "charged" all Staff members to respond to the committee's request. The LRPC chairman "charged" the Senior Pastor!

An initial draft followed which was then circulated to the various committees and commissions, and to our church staff to see how tolerable and/or possible the individual goals might be for our congregation. Needless to say there were endless refinements by all: some asking for more of this or less of that, some revising goals upwards or down, some calling attention to oversights, etc. etc. It was a productive and stimulating time to say the least. Almost everyone was "thinking" about our church and its commitment.

We were trying, of course, to bring everybody on board, rather than to have the Plan imposed by the staff or the "far-out" Long-Range Planning Committee. And, while "everybody" did *not* come on board "The Good Ship Long-Range", we were enthused by the response and never were deterred by the minimal resistance we received. We have often found a great idea derailed by a single critisism. Our committee was not so much hard-shell as hard-headed!

* * *

We believe that most lay people, young and old, male and female, would love to do more for the Church of Jesus Christ. We encourage church planners to look on officers and members as fellow travelers, rather than dead beat stick-in-the-muds who must be moved by force, not motivated by inclusion.

We discovered that when we set out meaningful things for lay people to do, they set out to do them and accomplished tremendous success. They felt better about the church, its ministry, and mission, and in the process, felt better about themselves as the people of God.

We do not recommend that you adopt the specifics of the following "Plan", unless, of course, you are in a similar position to where we think Southminster was when we developed the Plan. But this Plan might spark your committee to proceed with grace as well as gusto in moving your congregation forward. Good Luck and God Speed.

* * *

A FIVE YEAR PLAN FOR SOUTHMINSTER CHURCH

(Approved by the Session, November 1982)
(Revised and condensed for this book)

Introduction

It is said that if you do not know where you are going, any road will get you there. But, if you think you know where you want to be at some point in the future, then you might be able to chart a path that will help to get you there. That is the purpose of this plan.

I. The Strategic Mission

This is a plan to improve the quality and expand the scope of the ministry of Southminster Church. To accomplish this mission, an aggressive program and the commitment of the membership are the two most important factors.

II. Commissions and Boards

A. *Stewardship commission*—Responsible for stewardship commitment, mission interpretation, publicity, communications, etc.

1. Continue to develop and expand a program of education about the full meaning of stewardship and its practice on a continuous year-round basis.

2. Increase pledges by $100,000 per year by increasing the number of members pledging

from 80% to 90%, by increasing current number of member pledges, and by adding new members.

3. Pursue innovative methods of church financial giving and alternative means of church financing.

4. To develop an Endowment Fund to grow 35% per year.

B. *Nature and Fellowship Commission*—Responsible for adult programs, adult fellowship, small group development, Bible Studies, support groups, family health and concerns.

1. Provide a variety of programming opportunities to meet the needs and interests of the Adult members and to encourage participation in these programs on a community-wide basis. Specific new programs to be considered in the next five years are: women's ministries, men's work and mission, a network of small support groups, a variety of Bible studies, new member groups, young couples fellowship, Worship Plus One, etc.

2. Continue to coordinate the activities of the various adult groups within the church, i.e.: Adult Interest Center, Intercessors, Singles Group, Lay Callers, and Family Center, and to develop new programs, in line with the new needs.

C. *Christian Education Commission*—Responsible for Christian Education, Church School (adult and youth), and all other youth programs.

1. Develop an ongoing program of training for all church school and youth club teachers and leaders.

2. Provide educational programs for adults to meet varieties of needs as they are expressed; and increase adult participation by 10% per year.

3. Design and institute programs for educating parents and the congregation to help them deal with the growing problems of drug and alcohol abuse.

4. Include stewardship and mission education in the Christian Education program of our church, and expand opportunities for youth of all ages to participate in stewardship.

D. *Church and Community Commission*—Responsible for concerns of social righteousness, hunger relief, refugee family, Presbytery contact, ecumenical activities, and all *ad hoc* committees in the area of social rightousness.

1. Expand Southminster involvement in social action programs such as: Hunger Action Coalition, Jail Chaplaincy, Juvenile Offenders, Refugee Resettlement, and Drug Intervention Network, etc., to the extent that within five years, one out of ten members will have had such involvement.

2. Support the General Assembly's concentration on peacemaking, with a definitive program for Southminster involvement over the next ten years.

3. Become more active in ecumenical activities, both in our Community and beyond.

E. *Witness Commission*—Responsible for evangelism, new-member recruitment, development, etc.

1. Enroll a minimum 200 new members each year by an extensive public awareness campaign, by increased personal contact to promote awareness of Southminster programs, and by improved contact with new community residents.

2. Continually update the new member training courses and Seminars.

3. Cooperate with the Nurture and Fellowship Commission in their responsibility for assimilation of new members into the church.

F. *Operations Commission*—Responsible for operation of church property, staff concerns, long-range planning, and other duties of Trustees.

1. *Trustee*—The Trustees plan to carry out the routine maintenance necessary to keep the church properties in good condition and to accomplish at least the following major

items of renovation and maintenance in the next five years:

   a. Access for handicapped, including: the possibility of a ramp entrance (now realized), suitable handrails at some entrances, toilet facilities, etc.

   b. Energy savings: to insulate and protect stained glass windows, to implement heat utilization modifications.

   c. Establish a long-range program of specific maintenance projects, including: roof work, repointing, kitchen renovations, and parking lot resurfacing, etc.

2. *Personnel Committee*

   a. The increase of membership brings an increase in pastoral needs for calling and counseling. Other new and varied programs will require additional staff effort.

   b. To develop a program to provide opportunities for the professional staff to update its skills each and every year.

G. **Worship Commission**—Responsible for overseeing worship services, sacraments, music, fine arts, and drama.

1. Increase the average attendance at weekly worship services from the present 30% of membership to 50% within five years. (By June, 1987)

2. Have at least one major drama and musical each year, etc.

III. Boards and Organizations

A. *Deacons*—The office is one of sympathy and service, after the example of the Lord Jesus. Among other things: a Deacon shall minister to those in need, to the sick, to the friendless, to any who may be in distress, and help with new members.

1. Continue to provide a personal response to the needs of our members such as: lay calling, transportation, flower delivery, and other special projects.

2. Within the next three years, complete a program to seek out "inactive members", to determine the reasons for their inactivity, and to encourage their reinvolvement with Southminster.

B. ***Southminster United Presbyterian Women***—The Women's Association seeks to be obedient to God's call in Jesus Christ. They unite to support the Mission of the United Presbyterian Church in the United States, to help one another to grow in Christian faith and understanding, and to act in Christian concern in the company of God's people everywhere. They address themselves to:

1. The need to educate women to act both through prayer and political action on local, national, and international levels.

2. The need to emphasize mission: local, national, and international.

IV. Endowment Fund

Over the past five years, the Endowment Fund has grown from $85,000 to $350,000. It appears likely that it will grow at about $100,000 per year on an average over the next five years ($50,000 of which is new money). Thus, by the end of the five-year period, it is expected to be about $850,000. (By 1983, it was at $600,000.)

V. Membership and Financial Goals

In 1981, Southminster had about 2,350 members. (In 1963, we had 2,875.) The plan is to add 200 new members per year. With attrition expected because of deaths, members moving out-of-town, etc., this can be expected to increase membership a net of 70 members per year, or 350 for five years. Thus, in five years, Southminster should have 2,700 members provided it continues a very aggressive program to seek new members. (See Page A-10, Figure 1.)

Pledges to the regular church budget in 1981 totaled roughly $500,000. The Plan calls for pledges in five years totaling $1,000,000, an increase of $100,000 per year. This is an average increase of 15 percent per year. The new members should supply a net of about $15,000 per year after attrition from membership losses, leaving $85,000 per year average increase from continuing members, an average increase of about 12 percent per year. (Pledges for the 1983 church year were \$660,000.) Under this plan, the finances of the church in 1986 would be as follows:

REVENUE
Pledges....................	\$1,000,000
Endowment Income to Benevolences..............	50,000
Other Receipts (15% of Pledges)	150,000
Special Receipts (15% of Pledges)	150,000
	\$1,350,000

EXPENDITURES
Operating	\$ 790,000
Planned Maintenance	50,000
Radio, TV Fund	10,000
Benevolences................	350,000
Special Receipts	150,000
	\$1,350,000

Chapter VIII

THREE SAMPLE CASE STUDIES

To carry out its function, the LRPC should try to become familiar with as many facets as possible of the congregation's total activity. As we mentioned previously, many specific problems will arise in a church which do not clearly fall within the authority of any one of the established committees of the congregation. It is logical for the Session to delegate such concerns to the LRPC, and to ask them to take on the study of any such problem as an additional duty. It is difficult to classify a detailed list of such possible problems, but, as examples, we will note now three major concerns from the experience of Southminster Church in the years we were involved. There were countless other examples we could mention.

* * *

1. Our Church Owned Manse (Parsonage)

The terms of the original Call of our Senior Minister written in 1972, stated that, while he agreed to move into a church owned Manse, he had the right to ask for a "housing allowance" and to move out of the church owned home, whenever he and his family chose. After living in the Manse (as Presbyterians call it) for several years, the minister (and his wife) discovered that living in a huge residence across the parking lot from the main sanctuary had many disadvantages. In spite of the terms of his call, however, he

69

was reluctant to demand his contractural rights for fear that the process would become very expensive for the church and could also have caused severe objections and have hindered his work. The Southminster situation was complicated then by the fact that the Trustees, prior to the current minister's arrival, had completely remodeled the manse for the former Senior Pastor.

Several members were aware of the problem and called it to the LRPC's attention, who in turn (with Session approval) selected several people qualified in law, real estate, finance, construction etc. to serve as a "task group", to estimate the cost to the church of such a change, and other ramifications. The LRPC recommended to the Session that a proper and objective study be made. The Session approved.

After several meetings, the careful study revealed that the Manse, which was adjacent to the church building, could be used for other church purposes. Especially during those years when the cost of energy was becoming a paramount issue, we discovered that the main church building could be shut down at 5 P.M. and all evening meetings could be held at the house throughout the winter. The savings and convenience, (It had a porch the attendees could drive under in the cold or rainy weather.) largely offset the additional cost of the housing allowance. The LRPC in turn, suggested to the Session Personnel Committee that the Minister be given his original contractural housing allowance (plus some extra in light of inflation) in lieu of his residence in the Manse. The Session approved. The congregation was informed of the decision, and unanimously (2250 members) concurred (so far as we know). The terms of the original call were met at a moderate cost to all involved. The former Manse now houses Church School classes, committee meetings, needed storage space, youth programs, a guest apartment for visiting missionaries, a small apartment for one of the assistant ministers, etc. etc. All in all, everyone gained.

* * *

2. The Church Camp

In the early 1960's, Southminster received a tract of land in a rural area about fifty miles away from Mt. Lebanon from Mr. and Mrs. Donald Burnham. During that period of time (you might recall) many congregations were getting into what we call the "Camping Business". A fund-raising campaign was spearheaded by a beloved assistant minister, Rev. Harry Martin, which obtained enough money to build a central lodge, to remodel a huge barn, to level a ballfield, etc. etc. Presto, the congregation had a "Summer Home", Windy Ridge by name. The Session, Trustees, and Congregation approved the construction of the camp back then on the condition that the fees charged campers, and other income would cover operation costs. And, it was agreed (see the minutes) that once the building funds had been raised and spent the newly named Windy Ridge Camp would be self-supporting.

Shortly after the camp was operational, however, several major problems began to develop. First there was the lake, then the land-fill necessary, etc. etc. By the time we arrived, the particular problem was "water". After a group of a dozen or so people retreated to the Lodge for a long weekend, the well went dry! There was not even enough water for bathing and cooking for the remainder of that or the following several weekend retreats. This situation did not completely discourage the "teenagers" from using the camp, but parents and adults were forever looking elsewhere. And, with a change of church staff, and the changing ethos of the times, interest in the camp began to dwindle.

Numerous investigations by the committee assigned to supervise camp operations did research the problem and by scotch-tape and thumb-tack principle made do. It (soon) became clear, however, that it would require a large investment to solve the water problem. To buy, or pipe in water, or to build a storage tower, or . . . cost money. There was little chance that the congregation would authorize a fund-raising campaign to do this, what with all the needs and concerns at home and abroad. Consequently, a small underground storage tank was installed to cover immediate needs, so that water could be hauled in for short camping periods. Small groups could survive. But small groups do not a successful camping program make. Rarely was it feasible to charge large enough camping fees to cover ordinary expenses, let alone the cost of hauling or storing and pumping precious water. Greater use costs, the inconvenience of having to hoard water, which eventually evaporated off, caused potential users to decline the chance to rent the camp, as had been originally planned as a source of perennial income.

By the late 1970's (admittedly after some intentional neglect) the camp began to encroach upon the regular funds of the yearly church budget. Use of the camp by then was sporadic and infrequent, and the lodge and all of its appurtenances, were becoming old enough to need one after another repair. The Camp Committee was meanwhile responsible for "utilization of the camp" and for its program. The Church Trustees were responsible for maintenance and upkeep of the property. In between, as the poet said, the rest were drifting, to and fro. When our LRPC was asked to enter, there was no assigned entity to decide what the future of the camp should be.

The Session subsequently asked the LRPC to make a study and to advise what should be done about the camp. The LRPC proceeded to gather data. Its members interviewed church people, especially those who had been involved in the camp and its problems. The LRPC also cross-referenced to other congregational and synod camping programs, to see how our contemporaries handled the problem of a church owned camp. The results of these studies are briefly summarized in the preceeding paragraphs.

It was clear that there had been a strong trend among churches across the land to dispose of camps. It became clear that the continued operation of our particular camp would require some large expenditures, which would no doubt take away money from other church operations and benevolences. Finally, although not without disagreement, the continued operation of the camp was deemed to be unwise. The LRPC recommended that the Trustees be authorized to sell the land at the best price obtainable. (Soon, the whole issue became further complicated by problems of the mineral rights to the coal and gas beneath the surface of the camp property.)

We also found that there was a strong emotional involvement of many church members who had worked long hours in the original development of the camp. The Pastor, recognizing how faithfully the advocates had been, procrastinated the forward movement of the decision. The Session, also did not act promptly on the LRPC's recommendation. "Creative foot-dragging" (we call it) was going on, and on, and on. As a result, another study group was appointed.

After many meetings, where any and all church members were encouraged to express their views, the Session finally authorized the Trustees to sell the land and to put the proceeds into a permanent fund to promote youth activities and the general endowment of Southminster.

In the ensuing time, thanks to two young lawyer members of the church, the mineral rights problem was successfully solved and the camp property was listed on the market. Call the church to see what happened next!!

3. A Reorganization Of The Church Boards

From its inception in the late 1920's the Mt. Lebanon Presbyterian Church, later to become "Southminster", as many other of the Presbyterian churches of that vintage, was formed with three separate governing bodies. With little change, by the early 1970's the organization looked something like this:

(1) *THE SESSION*, consisting of 39 Elders and the Senior Minister as a non-voting Moderator and other clergy as members.

(2) *THE BOARD OF TRUSTEES*, consisting of 15 Trustees, with a slate of four elected officers, including the Church Treasurer, who controlled the funds.

(3) *THE BOARD OF DEACONS*, consisting of 30 Deacons with an Assistant or Associate Minister as a Moderator of the group.

In all three boards, members were elected for three-year terms of office, the Ruling Elders and Deacons at a congregational meeting and the Trustees at a Corporate Meeting, usually held immediately following the Congregational meeting. For all three, one-third of their membership was elected each year, with a total of twenty-eight *new* officers each and every year, joining the assembled ranks, eighty-four officers in all.

Every organization has its problems. For Southminster Church the most serious ones then generally came from too many committees, and too many spokes-people at too many meetings. The Session had dozens of committees, appointed over a period of years as needed, which were called upon to report each and every month. The Session had to hear all committee reports and, if necessary, act on their various recommendations. Monthly meetings were unbearably long. Talented men and women found excuses to miss the meetings, to leave early, or to refuse re-election. Power so diffused, is no power at all. Someone had selected a top-heavy approach to church government!

The Trustees at that time were responsible for the church properties, but had little authority to make effective decisions, because their every action required previous Session approval. A representative of the Trustees attended Session meetings, but still communication was inadequate, and often the Pastor found that he had to carry water on both shoulders, at once. At one point the Trustees threatened to resign *en masse,* because the Treasurer persuaded them that the Session was "putting them down".

Another problem was that Deacons in the old United Presbyterian Church were charged with "helping" other members, but the Deacons, too, had no authority at all to act on their own. Unless the Session delegated a responsibility, the office of Deacon tended to become a perfunctory one.

In the late 1970's the Senior Minister, with the approval of the Session, asked the LRPC to study the organizational arrangement and to determine if the operation of the boards could be made more efficient and effective in the work of the Gospel of Christ.

After lengthy discussions with current members of the three boards and considerable debate within its committee, the LRPC recommended that the three Boards be reduced into a single Session, the same to have a series of committees, one of which would take over the responsibilities of the former Trustees, another the responsibilities of the Deacons, but each would now be part of the Session. They would then have their authority to act, etc. When this proposal was debated in the Session and in open meetings of interested church members, it became clear that many members wanted the Board of Deacons kept separate from the Session. (We never did discover why.) So, the proposed re-organization was subsequently modified to continue a separate Board of Deacons. But the Session and the Trustees were merged into what in Presbyterianism we call a Unicameral Board. And, the Saints preserve us, at last look, it was still functioning.

Under the new organization, the Session consisted of thirty-three elected elders, with the Senior Minister serving as Moderator. Eleven members were to be elected each year. Of the eleven, six were assigned to the six commissions designated to accomplish the Six Great Purposes of the Presbyterian Church. (See the Presbyterian Form of Government, Preamble) Three members were to be designated Elder-Trustees. One extra member was assigned to the Church Operations Commission, and one was assigned the role of "Assistant Clerk" of the Session. Each Session member served on one commission for the three years, often, if not normally, becoming chairman the third year. Because of this reduction, the Session gained permanent strength over three years by electing only eleven members each year as eighteen retired.

All commissions are designed to be chaired by a current Session member, and the commissions have broad authority to carry out their responsibilities. They report monthly to the Session, and seek Session approval when required for their action. Most commissions are divided into committees. The committees report to the commissions. To give leeway to the commissions, we allowed that committee chairmen did not have to be members of the Session. The total number of lay participants of the Session, Commissions, Committees, and Deacons, at last count, numbered something over three hundred people: streamlined in organization for effective action and authority, yet with increased meaningful involvement. Dozens, and dozens, and dozens of new and competent people became involved all because of a revised organizational chart!

* * *

In the first year after the new organization was adopted, there were, of course, a few unpredictable problems, e.g., there was some overlapping responsibility in commission duties. A few items were accidently omitted. But these were easily resolved. Within a year it was clear that many of the problems of the old organization were gone, for good. All Trustees now attend Session meetings. Their authority and their actions derive from the same source. They can make their positions clear before decisions are reached, and they implement decisions which they helped to make.

As a by-product, with effective committee action, the long Session meetings were eliminated. Rarely, for two and one-half years, did a Session meeting last more than two hours. At one monthly meeting, where the commissions had truly done their work, the business was completed almost before the last member arrived. The Session meetings were rendered much more efficient. The details of the church's business were by design largely resolved in commission meetings, leaving the Session free to deal solely with the major issues of what it means to try to be the Church of Christ. The Session even began to take time for Bible Study, and when business meetings were shortened, they even began to get to know each other. A few of the more energetic even began to retire to the local "Eating Places" where fellowship reigned supreme.

Chapter IX

SOME TIPS FOR THE PASTOR
—a personal word

We have made it abundantly clear that we feel, you, the pastor-leader of the congregation are the key to the whole process of Long-Range Planning. We prefer to believe that the church does not "belong" to the minister. We honor the presence, and work for meaningful power for the elected lay leadership. We never referred to First Church as Macartney's Church. We each and all are part of the Church of Jesus Christ. We believe in the Role of the Laity. The Priesthood of ALL believers is not a token doctrine.

Neither, do we think that each and every item of the church's affairs should be under the 'key' direction of the minister. Most pastors we know do too much for and by themselves. The willingness or ability to delegate meaningful work for others is often lacking in even the most competent and capable of clergymen. There are prima donnas in a large percentage of Christian pulpits. Programmatic areas of finance, property development, even Christian education, and the Women's Association, the Altar Guild, ushers and greeters could each and all do just as well (and better!) without the guiding hand of the pastor. Learn to let go. The church was there when you arrived, and no doubt doing a job. We adore the epitaph which reads:

> Here lies our preacher, cold and killed.
> He tried to run the Ladies Guild!

Yet here, in setting the over-all Long-Range objectives for the congregation, we repeat again, there is no one else so essential as you, the Pastor. The Pastor has the over-view of the entire operation of the entire church. He/she alone is "called by God" to be responsible for that central leadership position. Even when a man (or woman) is appointed to the church by the Bishop, still, we have always believed the Will of God lies behind the directive to report to St. John's Church in Presbyterianville, Kentucky!

You, as Pastor, must see yourself as the one to whom the Planning finger points, with unerring direction. If you decide to sit on your hands when it comes to the particular course your congregation should pursue, then you (and they) will flounder about in whatever wind happens to be blowing at the time. If your personal travel calls for you to take a trip to Buffalo or Denver, then you must set out in the direction of New York or Colorado. Right? And even if you never manage to arrive, you will be heading in the right direction as you proceed.

You have been called to lead. If your goal is to be the Pastor of an all-round church in the area, you might never make it, but at least you will be pointing in that direction when your next call comes. We advise against looking for your next church while serving in this present one. Your congregation now deserves your total concentration. God will take care of their future (and your future as well), perhaps even in proportion to the way you plan and prosper where you are. Bloom where you are planted applies to Pastors, too.

Maybe you see your goal defined as ministering to the older citizens of your area, or to the youth, or to Ecumenical activity with the Catholics, or with the Jews or even the Baptists. In one extreme example, we know of, the Pastor's "Goal" was to merge the congregation with another and close the doors for good. Whatever your goals might be, you must set out in that direction, or you will never get there, wherever that direction is. God's Will allows for a variety of specific courses. Occasionally, if not often, we are prone to seek the wrong one, but "no direction at all" is the worst offense of them all! The church which takes the risk of a new direction sometimes picks the wrong one. The church which never does, will forever be "right", but it will be forever the same.

You, as Pastor, are responsible to chart the course. Be attentive, of course, to the people you are called to serve. The crew can be of tremendous help. The Holy Spirit can work wonders wherever you are. Try to understand the past and present of the congregation. But, do not forfeit your leadership to the prophets, the historians, or the futurists. God has a special place for all. Be a key which can unlock the future. It takes work: hard thinking, praying, planning, working. Almost always you will proceed without a complete unanimity of the voices deep inside. (To say little of the lack of unanimity of the voices outside!) But to move without full knowledge (getting back to Abraham in whom we, by the way, enormously believe) is to be a child of God. Think enough about your parish to offer it your brains as well as your pastoral energy and preaching excellence; and, having done it all, get up and go!

Tips For The Pastor

I. Before we offer a few practical tips, there is this preliminary one. Back on the Frontispiece we included the words from Proverbs which read: "Many are the plans in the mind of man, but it is the purpose of the Lord that will be established". (Proverbs 19:21) That is just an initial way of reminding ourselves that the Church does not belong to the Long-Range Planning people. Neither does it belong to the Pastor, or the Session! It belongs to the One who formed it, the One who gave it life, to the One who loves it in spite of all its faults and frailities.

We urge you to begin the Long-Range Planning process, as each and every other process of your church's dreams, in the spirit of humility and private prayer. The Guidance of the Holy Spirit is promised and available. In all of the times and techniques we have learned, none comes in even a close second to the Power we felt in knowing we were seeking to find God's Will and to find the courage to carry it out. Be prayerful. Listen to the depth of your own soul and to the power and presence of the Christ who lives within you. That is what will separate you from the others. That is the only way you will become His Church.

II. With that beginning, then we go on to say: "*Plan yourself*". We became aware, as we proceeded through the several opening years of this effort at Southminster, that we were calling on each and every officer and committee to think through their plans for the future. Some responded wisely, some responded well. It later occurred to us (and one of "us" was the Senior Pastor) that we had not called upon *The Staff* to plan their future, —a careless oversight to be sure, of the highest possible danger.

Ministers normally, we have found, are not great (or even good) at planning their weeks, to say nothing of their days and decades. (Incidentally we often discovered that their wives do indeed "plan" very well.) We recommend that the LRPC (in love) call upon the Minister and other staff members, to address a long-range goal. Personal development, professional advancement, changing styles of ministry, new directions *et al* are part of what we discovered was lacking in our staff. They got so busy doing, they forgot what they were supposed to do, the better their virtue, the less their vision.

Even the dullest pastors among us are capable of magnificent improvement if prodded carefully and without malice. We never met a scatter-brained minister who did not desire to get organized, if he only knew how and found the motivation. Our LRPC helped our pastor. The first practical tip is that *"You must Plan yourself"*. Possibly you will be able to attend a good planning seminar. You might then read all the material you can find. But do not fail to renew yourself in the process of renewing others. The "Captain" must know the way, or the ship will never arrive at its desired haven.

III. *Do not become discouraged!* Your church with all its problems and possibilities, was most likely there long before you came. It will no doubt be there long after you are gone. God himself made the universe in seven short days. But, never be misled into thinking that you and I can do the same. Actually (we believe) it took God eons and eons of time to get us to this moment. But we do not have eons either.

Look for progress, not completion. Reinhold Neibuhr once cautioned that nothing we hope to do worth doing can ever be accomplished in one lifetime, let alone in one pastorate, so we must learn to live on hope. You must depend upon your successor, as your predecessor now has to depend upon you. Frederick Douglas once warned that no change ever comes without violence. He was speaking on the broad range of civic affairs. But resistance is normal and necessary. If you are not willing to fight for what you believe, perhaps you do not believe it enough. And, if you prefer not to be worried by the admonitions of a Civil Rights leader, be cheered by the timeless old lady who confessed privately to her pastor, "Oh, I'm in favor of progress", she whispered. "It is all these changes I can't stand!"

IV. *Be open with the membership.* We have found the almost incessant need for pastors and priests to see themselves in opposition to the laity. The "enemy" becomes the poor misguided layman who happens to disagree (honest disagreement we might add) with the clergyman. We know one pastor who categorized an elder on the basis of one comment, long ago forgotten by the layman. We encourage you to think of the laity of your congregation as God's servants: sons and daughters who are brothers and sisters, as you are, with God's only son, Jesus.

There can be, and have to be, disagreements in almost every family. If the Church is The Family of God, unanimity will not occur. Beware when all men speak well of you. Beware more if all women ever do! But, honesty has its own reward. If you are pleased with a particular program and practice, let everyone know. Brag about the good work of your committees or your staff. If you are unhappy with any item of property, program, or person, be gentle, be loving, but be open to let your key leadership know what must happen before you can move it all forward.

One day, way back in Seminary, our Professor of Christian Education was asked: "But, what can you do when you inherit a Sunday School Superintendent who is incompetent, but who has been there for forty-six years?" You will not believe what we learned from the answer: "Pray for a funeral", he jested. Everybody laughed and so we hope will you. But in the long view, change comes in long and painful doses. It is your job to be the Doctor.

This is all a way of saying that occasionally (if not often) the pastor will be caught in difficult situations.

You can ease it all by sharing your goals. First you must have them, but we encourage you to be decisive. We often say that if the minister chooses not to "run" the church, he must be sure that no one else "chooses to run" it either. Be honest with the crew. We do recall the captain who reassuring them all in the middle of a huge and awful tempest, said "I assure you everything will be alright . . . provided the whole ship doesn't split down the middle!"

V. But equally, *keep some few secrets to yourself.* Everyone deserves a fine and private place: in marriage, in business, in churches, etc. Sometimes visionaries disturb other people around them. Therefore you will need to move a little slower than you might choose at first. But, Rome was not built in a day, and, it took the Lord a long, long time to get you together with His Church. We feel certain that He can wait a little longer for the Kingdom really to come. You arrive, as Arthur Gossip once said, "punctually on time". The Lord has work for you to do, now.

Most good leaders keep their followers guessing, some times. Suspense helps creativity and avoids having to do useless battle from the start. The power of God's Spirit can work through a multitude of people, and, who knows, if the pastor does not demand an immediate acceptance of what he, or she, thinks, then the pastor might learn a little too. We hope. In either case there will always be another meeting to bring it up again. One of our predecessor Senior Ministers was often accused of using the "Tabled Motion" to bring it up at a later meeting, when the dissidents were gone.

We have found through the years that if a leader exposes too much too early, opposition will build up to a "Plan". If your view is looking ahead five or even ten years, there is little need to exert tremendous pressure for immediate change, but, if you have the "right" plan, (Our efforts here are designed to help you unearth the "rightness" of your plan.) then others catch on as you go. We knew one Elder once who declared himself to be a "preacher's man". He often began his comment by saying he wanted what the preacher wanted, but since he seldom knew what the "Preacher" wanted, he often went on to declare in favor of the opposite.

One thing we know for sure from our experience is that the Pastors themselves, to say nothing of our laity, are capable of tremendous change. We never say, "I told you so". (Or rather we try not to say it; or to say it in the most subtle way we can.) But we have often heard by now, a stranger to our point some years ago, expounding it currently with vigor, forgetting, that he or she (normally he) opposed it with equally vociferous vigor, some months or years before. If you can make "your" idea, "their" idea, you have found the salient secret of success. Halleluiah! Amen.

VI. The sixth tip is borrowed from the sports-minded world in which we live. Whether it be soccer, tiddily-winks, or the 400 metered hurdles, the constant charge is *"Keep your eye upon the goal"*. We do not think it is inappropriate for the pastor to adopt the image of the leader. Someone needs to be the Chairman of the Board. Every ship needs a captain. Every battalion needs a commander, especially in battle. And while the clergy need to be refined in the burning fires of movement, to say nothing of the corrective fires of God, still the Pastor is called to be responsible for "vision". Where there is no vision, the Bible says, the people perish still. The Pastor must provide the vision, call the people to greatness, or at least call them to greater things. Your ministry and Christ's Mission will rejoice.

We have found that successful pastors always have a cache of new ideas, always know what should be done. If someone arrives one day and says: "I have a million dollars for the Church", the pastor should be able to respond: "Good, this is how we will spend it". Or, if someone comes to say: "I need something more to do", the pastor needs to say, "Fine, here are five things we need". Etc. Etc.

You see if the pilot of the plane does not know the destination, then the poor people in the seats will never get there. You must know already where they want to go, if you are called of God. They want to find the guidance of the life in Christ the Scripture offers them. They want to find eternal peace. They want harmony in their homes. They want their children to succeed. They want to feel their service to Christ is useful. They are not trying to earn salvation; they are trying to do a good job. They need to know that the love of God shines upon their efforts. And, they want their Church to succeed. They want to feel good about their membership.

That is the destination. If the pastor is not committed to that voyage, he should go and sell insurance. Christian people need to know the way to go. If the pilot does not know the way, they will crash upon the seen and unseen rocks and rills.

If the pastor does his job, if some time is saved for planning, if he takes a walk upon the mountain and catches the great view and vision which rolls on out before him, then, oh dearie me . . . the Church of Christ might really change the world. And the day will come "when justice will roll down like the waters, and righteousness will come like an ever-flowing stream. Then you shall go out with joy and be led forth in peace," it says, "and the mountains and hills shall break forth before you into singing and all the trees in the field shall clap their hands."

We have no other tips, not just now anyway. But Christ will see you through it all. Honestly He will. And to that, we hope, that you might add a great A-MEN. Peace and love to you through Jesus Christ our Lord.

CONCLUSION

In brief outline form, we present as a final summary, the intent and content of this book:

1. The Church which does not plan its future, and does not seek to anchor the whole activity down to some chosen direction, will be carried along by whatever wind is blowing, or worse, drift about forever in the same little coves of yesterday, protected to be sure, but missing the grand high journey of what it means to be and to become the people of Jesus Christ our Lord.

2. The Scripture, and especially the teachings of Jesus, while calling us forever to the worries of the present, and encouraging us to live the abundant life to its fullest today, (for we know not what another day might bring forth), still directs us, by example and precept, to plan the work and worship of our individual lives, and the life we share in the church.

3. The Long-Range Planning can best be conducted when a chosen Committee is selected and set free to do its task. The chairman and the committee members, along with the Pastor and Ruling Body, should move slowly and carefully to develop:

    a. A Planning Guide
    b. A Statement of Purpose
    c. A Plan For Specific Actions
    d. A Follow-up System for Review

4. The Long-Range Planning Committee should be charged with involving *all* the elected officers through the various committees, commissions, as well as the professional church staff in the Long-Range Planning task, then the membership at large. It should be the driving force to see that the others move to a chosen future. Care and kindness for different opinions are paramount, but someone in the congregation must seek to set the course which lies ahead.

5. The Long-Range Planning Committee can (should) with proper delegated authority, adopt some special projects as its own and carry out the work, especially in areas which do not easily "belong" to some existing committee, or areas so wide in range that they cross over several assigned responsibilities.

6. We believe the Pastor (or the Senior Pastor in a large church staff) is the key to successful Long-Range Planning. It is an area he/she should not delegate to someone else. The Pastor's enthusiasm for the project and his energy devoted to it, will be the determining factor in the effectiveness of the Long-Range Planning of your congregation.

7. God will guide you as you go, through the power, peace and presence of His Spirit, for now and Evermore.

APPENDIX A

Some Sample Pages for and from
"A Planning Guide"

From:

Trends Affecting the Southminster Presbyterian
Church
A Guide for Planning—June 1980 by
the Long-Range Planning Committee

MT. LEBANON, PENNSYLVANIA

(The Community in which
Southminster Church is located)

A. Population

The population of Mt. Lebanon in 1970 was
39,596, based on Census Bureau statistics. The
data for the 1980 census are expected to be available
by April, 1981. While past projections have
indicated a potential growth in population in Mt.
Lebanon to the level of 45,000, recent trends,
both nationally and locally, now imply a declining
population during the present decade, 1980-
1990.

Year	Population	% Increase (Decrease) Per Decade
Actual:		
1920	2,258	—
1930	13,403	—
1940	19,571	46.0
1950	26,604	35.9
1960	35,361	32.9
1970	39,596	12.0
1979	35,664	—
Forecast:		
1980	34,366*	(13.2)
1985	31,600	—
1990	28,865	(16.0)

*1980 Census preliminary result.

The above decreases are a result of dramatically lower birth rates based upon such factors as prolonged educational trends, more effective birth control techniques, and various economic and environmental concerns, all contributing to a considerable shift in national attitudes. In addition, Mt. Lebanon itself has relatively few major segments of undeveloped land available for growth in dwelling units.

Population by Zone. Some shift in population distribution by tract within Mt. Lebanon is forecast, with increases in the South-central zones exceeding the average. This is a result of availability of open development land and increases in multi-family dwelling units. The maximum loss can be expected in the central zone due to aging of available housing stock and increases in commercial development.

B. Population by Age Group

By far the most significant changes to be anticipated, both from the area standpoint and its implications to Southminster, lie in the area of notable shifts in the make-up of the age groupings comprising total population. Age-group distribution changes of the magnitude of ± 20% are forecast between 1970 and 1980 in age group distribution. Specifically, the school-age population for Mt. Lebanon (up to 19), unlike some of the national trends, is expected to decrease dramatically over the decade, dropping from 9482 to an estimated 6360 by 1990, a 33% decline. Statistics presently available from the school district tend to validate the trend. An equally dramatic increase in the age group between 20 and 44 is expected, reflecting the post-World War II "baby boom." Finally, as would be anticipated, the trend toward a larger proportion in the over 65 group will continue.

C. Education & Employment

Education. Based on 1970 statistics, the median educational level for residents of Mt. Lebanon, aged 24 and over, was 13.4 years. Level of education was as follows:

Population Over 25 by Years of School Completed

1. High School or less	47.84%
2. 1-3 years of college	17.28%
3. 4 or more years of college	34.85%

Past trends have resulted in an increase of college educated residents, growing from approximately 25% in 1960 to the present 34.85%. While cultural and economic considerations could cause some variation in current trends, this proportion could reasonably be expected to approach 40 to 45% during the 1980's. In contrast, it will be recalled, for the nation as a whole only 20 percent of people in the 25 to 29 year-old group were college graduates.

Employment. Surveys conducted in 1970 give the following breakdown of major occupational classifications:

Professional and
Technical 32.57%
Managers and
Administrative 18.94%
Sales 13.82%
Clerical . . . . <u>18.10%</u>

Total "White Collar" 83.43%
Crafts, Operations, Labor
Services, Domestic 16.57%

No significant changes in the above distribution would be indicated in the foreseeable future.

D. Income

The decade of the 1960's showed an increase in median family income in Mt. Lebanon of approximately 35%, from $10,000/year to $13,500/year. This increase, during a period of relatively stable economic conditions, represented a growth rate around 3% per year. Since the late 60's, the expansion has accelerated primarily due to inflationary trends, with relatively little increase in "real dollar" growth. For the period 1970-1980, an increased range closer to 8% per year can, therefore, be anticipated, barring any major economic crises. On this assumption, median family income can be expected to approach $24,000 per year by 1980 and continue higher to near the $53,000 level by 1990.

Table VI

SOUTHMINSTER PRESBYTERIAN
CHURCH MEMBERSHIP

Year	Deaths	Losses Transfers	Removal	Total	New Members	Net Change	Membership Year-End
1963	—	—	—	—	—	—	2,826
1964	22	125	8	155	173	+18	2,844
1965	18	131	19	168	155	−13	2,831
1966	23	110	16	149	155	+6	2,837
1967	30	89	12	131	141	+10	2,847
1968	26	97	421	544	139	−405	2,442
1969	30	103	181	314	147	−167	2,275
1970	22	83	7	112	90	−22	2,253
1971	44	43	285	372	46	−326	1,927
1972	24	62	0	86	128	+42	1,969
1973	25	51	7	84	142	+58	2,027
1974	26	69	3	98	120	+22	2,049
1975	23	37	0	60	147	+87	2,136
1976	24	34	0	58	217	+159	2,295
1977	24	40	0	64	136	+72	2,367
1978	28	51	194	273	123	−152	2,217
1979	35	44	0	79	91	+12	2,229

Table XI

PLEDGING RECORD
SOUTHMINSTER PRESBYTERIAN CHURCH

Year	Number Pledges Received	Pledges In- creased	Pledges Equaled	Pledges De- creased	Pledges New Mem- bers	Total Amount Received	Average Pledge
1950	791	251	411	42	87	$104,970.	$136.
1951	906	289	477	48	92	116,907.	129.
1952	893	328	457	40	68	129,685.	145.
1953	925	218	560	68	79	131,286.	141.
1954	916	196	612	43	65	137,139.	149.
1955	869	144	622	44	59	131,538.	151.
1956	889	362	434	30	63	149,061.	176.
1957	935	452	349	50	84	171,616.	187.
1958	943	414	392	71	66	192,161.	212.
1959	924	321	476	83	44	212,676.	229.
1960	954	432	428	44	50	243,262.	255.
1961	928	304	486	81	57	260,773.	281.
1962	924	196	561	114	53	253,901.	275.
1963	940	225	592	58	65	256,891.	273.
1964	880	379	416	36	49	270,276.	307.
1965	861	288	475	63	35	265,192.	308.
1966	833	304	439	53	37	263,829.	316.
1967	803	343	389	43	28	281,712.	350.
1968	738	159	493	69	17	264,363.	358.
1969	672	261	327	56	28	269,326.	400.
1970	704	327	323	44	20	304,083.	427.
1971	643	164	386	88	5	288,622.	450.
1972	577	165	348	63	1	269,439.	467.
1973	632	332	248	26	26	307,193.	486.
1974	627	248	312	48	19	308,509.	492.
1975	624	312	262	40	10	304,922.	489.
1976	624	346	229	38	11	328,124.	524.
1977	697	336	228	46	37	370,736.	531.
1978	661	320	288	37	16	389,237.	588.
1979	689	289	339	61	30	416,529.	604.

Table X

TOTAL DOLLARS RECEIPTS
SOUTHMINSTER PRESBYTERIAN CHURCH

| Year | Member-ship | Current Receipts | | Sub-Total | Special Receipts | Total |
		Oper.	Benev-olences			
1925	200	9,442	778	10,220	202	10,422
1926	252	9,482	1,684	11,166	4,858	16,024
1927	341	9,966	1,567	12,511	73,914	85,447
1928	468	13,340	688	14,028	14,338	28,366
1929	496	17,892	2,316	20,208	14,015	34,223
1930	560	20,171	1,861	22,032	6,556	28,588
1931	631	20,875	2,500	23,375	4,108	27,543
1932	652	13,879	1,692	15,571	1,240	16,811
1933	767	15,824	1,864	17,688	185	17,873
1934	813	16,035	2,218	18,253	2,829	21,082
1935	888	16,230	2,500	18,730	2,650	21,380
1936	963	16,263	2,837	19,100	2,498	21,598
1937	982	17,461	2,947	20,408	1,728	22,136
1938	1,081	18,160	2,117	20,277	1,050	21,327
1939	1,103	19,884	2,535	22,419	1,514	23,933
1940	1,156	20,417	4,191	24,608	1,558	26,166
1941	1,169	18,663	2,765	21,428	7,955	29,383
1942	1,342	23,819	3,498	27,317	3,480	30,797
1943	1,580	30,580	4,022	34,602	9,889	44,491
1944	1,931	38,264	7,841	46,105	3,399	49,504
1945	1,934	35,475	8,226	43,701	54,886	98,587
1946	2,003	45,395	12,395	57,790	13,651	71,441
1947	2,115	56,637	10,672	67,309	7,143	74,452
1948	2,129	59,655	23,514	83,169	18,848	102,017
1949	2,340	53,414	22,340	75,754	36,536	112,290
1950	2,493	58,712	23,567	82,279	43,169	125,448
1951	2,543	107,595	23,044	130,639	23,477	154,116
1952	2,563	118,279	28,682	146,961	27,587	174,548
1953	2,595	119,338	31,336	150,674	24,218	174,892
1954	2,604	85,637	40,910	126,547	77,496	204,016

(Continued)

A-8

Table X

TOTAL DOLLARS RECEIPTS
SOUTHMINSTER PRESBYTERIAN
CHURCH (Continued)

| Year | Member-ship | Current Receipts | | Sub-Total | Special Receipts | Total |
		Oper.	Benev-olences			
1955	2,650	119,171	43,259	162,430	56,363	218,793
1956	2,777	121,617	56,373	177,990	59,498	237,488
1957	2,694	122,106	56,704	178,810	60,535	239,345
1958	2,764	139,800	64,893	204,693	63,584	268,277
1959	2,852	168,006	74,076	242,082	30,349	272,431
1960	2,879	146,056	87,237	233,293	40,439	273,732
1961	2,915	156,871	96,392	253,263	79,111	332,374
1962	2,930	144,389	99,196	243,585	61,759	305,344
1963	2,826	178,607	94,807	273,414	61,315	334,729
1964	2,844	192,343	111,790	304,133	57,121	361,254
1965	2,831	206,595	93,960	300,555	40,645	331,200
1966	2,837	201,109	85,909	287,018	33,303	320,321
1967	2,847	214,710	137,218	351,928	112,410	464,338
1968	2,442	178,691	133,429	312,120	91,370	403,850
1969	2,275	232,677	117,690	350,367	88,292	438,659
1970	2,253	249,040	113,408	362,448	44,497	406,945
1971	1,927	220,821	113,898	334,719	82,649	417,368
1972	1,969	241,326	96,856	338,182	19,721	357,903
1973	2,027	293,334	86,026	379,360	35,334	414,694
1974	2,049	285,254	88,745	373,999	44,602	418,601
1975	2,136	304,573	81,264	385,837	55,470	441,307
1976	2,295	309,459	83,709	393,168	61,143	454,311
1977	2,367	331,236	81,306	412,542	71,452	483,994
1978	2,217	392,689	82,379	475,068	97,958	573,026
1979	2,229	437,126	83,000	520,126	297,413	817,539

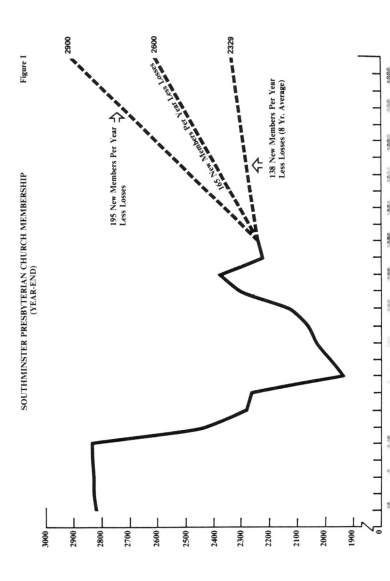

SOUTHMINSTER PRESBYTERIAN CHURCH MEMBERSHIP
(YEAR-END)

Figure I

195 New Members Per Year
Less Losses

2900

165 New Members Per Year Less Losses

2600

138 New Members Per Year
Less Losses (8 Yr. Average)

2329

A-10

APPENDIX B

SOUTHMINSTER PRESBYTERIAN CHURCH
A Revised Statement of Purpose—1980
(condensed for present volume)

We the people of Southminster Church declare our basic purpose to be the fulfillment of the obligations, the duties, and the privileges of being a Christian church and more especially a particular congregation of the United Presbyterian Church (USA), of which Jesus Christ is the sole and only head. Without intending to exclude appreciation for or cooperation with other churches and denominations, and without failing to give concrete expression to the same, we do acknowledge our responsibilities to be active partici- pants in the connectional forms of the United Presby- terian government. We are aware as a congregation that His church consists of all those persons in every nation, together with their children, who make profes- sion of the Christian religion and submit to His guidance.

With Christ as the Head of the Church, and we as His servant people, gathered together in the Presbyte- rian form of government, we acknowledge the Scrip- tures to be our rule of faith and practice and the underlying source of our guidance and direction. We believe in the Mission which is mandated by the

Scripture. We believe in the effective power of God's word to guide us.

Believing this, we begin our Statement of Purpose by adopting the Six Great Ends of the Church as acknowledged in the Book of Order of our demonination, to be the basis of our Session organization.

I. The Proclamation of the Gospel for the Salvation of Humankind

In the Christian faith, "Proclamation" has always meant the preached word. We continue to affirm that usage, but this Commission is concerned also with the response of the people of our church to the Word. The responsibility includes lay involvement, Stewardship Commitment, year-round mission interpretation, publicity, communications, and ecumenical matters.

II. The Shelter, Nurture and Fellowship of the Children of God

We seek to be the Church in which all believers, regardless of age or sex or marital status or politics or theological stance, are welcome to belong to the fellowship. We seek to be servants of God's love in the families where we live, and in the broader family of our church; to show our love for each other in the way we care in times of need. We seek opportunities to break down the loneliness and isolation of our time and to bring people together beyond their different ages and interests, including ecumenical encounters with those outside our Presbyterian way.

III. The Maintenance of Divine Worship

We promise to provide for the worship of our gathered members and our guests in the preaching of His word, in prayer and sacrament, in a variety of worship experiences which hold the old and new together. We believe that in worship Jesus Christ confronts humanity in order that they may be moved by the Holy Spirit to respond in adoration, humility and repentance. We believe that in public worship, God makes known his love in Christ, His claim upon our lives, His abiding presence and His concern for all creation.

IV. The Preservation of the Truth

We seek to be an articulate and informed congregation. We promise to provide accepted Christian Education to people of all ages, and we seek to keep our educational process in the central place of all we do. We promise to provide facilities and leadership where the Spirit of God can work His will and way. We emphasize a proper knowledge of the Scripture and its major ways and themes. We seek to be sure that what is taught to the youngest child is consistent with the knowledge of the mature young adult. We promise to use whatever media and methods can best communicate the message, and seek to be a dedicated community of God's people, preserving and honoring His truth, and being led by it.

V. The Promotion of Social Righteousness

We believe that in Jesus Christ God was reconciling the world to Himself. The life, death, resurrection and promised coming of Jesus Christ sets the pattern for our Mission. Because we believe that God has created the people of the earth to be one universal family, we strive to overcome every form of discrimination. The Church is called to bring all Christians to uphold each other as persons in all the relationships of life, in employment, housing, education, leisure, marriage, family, church, and the exercise of political rights. We promise to defend the needy and the exploited and to adopt the cause of the world's poor and hungry as our own. We promise to work for peace in our community, in our nation and throughout the world. We adopt the promotion of social righteousness as a primary goal of what Southminster Presbyterian Church intends to do and believe.

VI. The Exhibition of the Kingdom of Heaven to the World

We seek no higher praise or purpose than the Biblical commendation, "By this shall all men know that you are my disciples, that you have love one for another". We believe in evangelism, which means "glad tidings". We promise to try to live with such conviction in witnessing to our purposes that others around us will see us, know who we are, and whom we seek to serve. Our evangelism then is to convince, not to coerce, to share the tidings of great joy, by example of who we are and what we do.

THE AUTHORS

Warren B. Davis

An Active "Sooner" from Muskogee, Oklahoma, Warren graduated from Tulsa University and joined Gulf Oil Corporation just in time to be sent off to spend the next four years in the United States Air Force. He returned to Tulsa and was eventually transferred to the Corporate headquarters of Gulf, in Pittsburgh, Pennsylvania. Mr. Davis recently retired from his position of Chief Economist of Gulf Oil. Most of his 40 plus years were spent in corporate Planning.

As a high ranking official, and busily involved at the national level in Governmental matters related to energy issues, Mr. Davis still maintained an extraordinary commitment to his church. He taught Junior High classes for thirty years. At Southminster Church in Mt. Lebanon, Pennsylvania, he was ordained as Elder and accepted an early assignment on the Long-Range Planning Committee. More years than not, he was Chairman of the Committee. Warren currently lives in Kitty Hawk, North Carolina, and is a member of the Outer Banks Presbyterian Church.

Dr. Cromie is currently Senior Pastor of the First Presbyterian Church of Fort Lauderdale, Florida. From 1972 to 1983 he was at Southminster Presbyterian Church in Mount Lebanon, Pennsylvania, where he was pastor and friend to Warren Davis. The book was a joint effort. The substance came from Mr. Davis; the additional work from Dr. Cromie. Dr. Cromie is also the author of *"Sometime Before the Dawn:* Responses to the Resurrection"; and a published booklet: *"How To Live With Cancer".* Both are available through Desert Ministries, Inc. He is proud to be co-author of this present volume.